Fly Casting:
A Systematic Approach

Sheila M. Hassan

Published by Cast90.com
Lulu Press
P.O. Box 617
Medway, Ma 02053
www.Cast90.com
Copyright © 2009…. by Sheila M. Hassan
ISBN # 978-0-578-10746-2

Printed in the United States of America

Sheila and Bill Hassan
Cast90.com
FFF Master Certified Casting Instructors

Fly Casting:
A Systematic Approach

Sheila M. Hassan

Photos by Bill Hassan

Contents

Acknowledgments

Thanks to my best friend and husband, Bill. His encouragement and patience are amazing. No one ever achieves their goals without the support of those around them, and I have been fortunate to have Bill. He has helped me in so many ways and I could not achieve what I have, without his love and support. I am also lucky that he is the best fishing and teaching partner anyone could hope to have. Thank you!

I would also like to thank the many generous people who served as my casting mentors. They spent invaluable time and effort with me. Patiently listening to my questions and working with me to improve my understanding and skills. This starts with George Roberts who gave me my first formal casting lesson. He openly admits I was his best student not because of skill, but for my tenacity and willingness to work hard. George set me on a great learning adventure about casting. I am fortunate to have continued my casting development by working and studying under Floyd Franke and Joan Wulff. A special thanks to Bruce Richards, Dusty Sprague, Gordy Hill, as well as many other Federation of Fly Fishers casting board of governors who have helped influence my casting and teaching. I am also thankful for the industry support I have had over the years. Thanks to: Justin and Parker Sterner from R.L. Winston Rods, and Scientific Anglers fly lines; Brad Gage from Sage rods; Bob Lamson from Ross Reels and Ross Worldwide; Jake Jakespeare from Temple Fork Outfitters; Don Barnes from Regal Vise; Diane Bristol and Andy Wunsch from Simms; Bill Kline from Patagonia. In addition, I thank my local fly fishing shops, which have supported me over the years including: Scott, Sarah and Amanda from the Bear's Den in Taunton; Vinny from Natick Outdoor Sports; and Nat and Derek from First Light Anglers in Rowley. Lastly, I want to thank all of my students over the past 10 years, you are my inspiration for continuing to teach and to strive to make this sport more fun for others.

How to use this book

This book is not intended to be the final word or bible on fly casting. Rather it represents the concepts that I believe are important for a caster as they progress from beginner to advanced, in a lesson format. Unfortunately, we fly casters expect to be able to naturally fly cast. Fly casting is not a natural action and most people need instruction and coaching to improve.

This book represents my version of beginner, intermediate and distance casting skills. I humbly offer this book to be useful to students of casting. I have nothing new to offer about the physics of fly casting. It has not fundamentally changed over the years. There is still a roll cast and basic cast (a back and forward cast) the techniques of shooting line, false casting, and the double haul. Everything else in fly casting is a variation or adaptation of this core set of skills. What I can offer is a different perspective of how to present the information. This is my take on the concepts. I hope to relate them to you in a way that makes sense and works for you. The book is a compilation of my experiences as a student and teacher. We are all products of the people who have helped us in our lives, and the same is true for my casting life. I have spent much of my time with Joan Wulff and George Roberts. Their influence and that of other great casters is woven throughout this book. The more you can learn from others, the richer you will be in the end.

The three lessons in this book represent phases of your casting life. The material is not intended to be experienced as three lessons over three consecutive weekends. Rather it should be used over the phases of your fishing career. You start as a beginner then proceed to intermediate level casting and its challenges. Over time, you gain experience fishing. Finally, whether as a measure of personal success or as needed for fishing, most casters eventually find themselves seeking to improve their distance casting. These are the core lessons, which most casters need.

The second part of this book focuses on practice. I feel strongly that this is the key factor that determines your casting ability. Practice is critical to your skill improvement. Committing to dedicated practice time was the turning point in my own casting improvement. I cannot stress enough the importance of practice. The practice section has both exercises and detailed lists of how to evaluate each cast. You can start at any point and focus on the skill most important to you at that time. You can return later (months or years) and focus on additional skills.

The book is not all-inclusive or exclusive. However, it does present sufficient material to last for several years, and could serve as a reference for a lifetime. The intention is for you to use the book repeatedly as you improve your skills and increase your goals. Even if you are an experienced caster, I encourage you to review the material in the introductory lesson. This is where your fundamental body movements for the cast are explained in detail and the fundamental concepts of efficient fly casting are developed.

Part I- Fly Casting Lessons

Lesson 1: Introduction to Fly Casting: Building Solid Fundamentals

Introduction

Fly casting the unique sport

Many people interested in fly casting attempt to learn to cast on their own. Because it is fishing, they believe they should be capable of teaching themselves to cast and it should be intuitive. Frequently, they get frustrated early in their learning because the body movements needed to make a good fly cast are not like other sport actions they have learned. This frustration with the casting is why many people abandon their dreams of fly fishing and just give up. If you take the time and learn to cast, you will have far greater success and enjoy this sport.

How is fly casting different from other sports? There are two main differences. In conventional fishing, you are casting a lure or bait which has its weight in a concentrated form. Your action is to bring the rod back to set up for a strong forward throw. You are casting the weight of the lure or bait and the monofilament fishing line is pulled off the reel by this weight. In fly casting the weight you are casting is a long flexible weight in the form of your fly line. The fly is a passenger and is delivered to the target by the fly line. You are not directly throwing your fly toward the fish. You are creating a loop that will deliver the fly for you. The second way that fly casting is different from other sports is that you have a back cast. The back cast is not simply a maneuver to set up for the forward cast. The back cast is a cast unto itself and is every bit as important as the forward cast. Fly casting is unique in this need for a backward throwing maneuver. Since most people are not conditioned to throw backwards, this is one of the main challenges in fly casting.

What is the essence of fly casting?

The goal of fly casting is making open ended unrolling loops which deliver your fly to the fish. You are an intermediary. Your role is to cast the loop of fly line and allow the loop to deliver the fly to the target. You do not try to throw the fly. Instead, focus on creating the loop which aimed properly, will unroll delivering your fly to the target area. It is the fly line, which propels your fly to the target. Therefore, the loop is the central focus of fly casting. Stealth and finesse are involved in fly casting. Stealth in your presentation to make your hook and feathers appear attractive to the fish, and finesse in the way you cast your line so the fly is in the correct place and looks natural to the fish. This is what makes fly casting both an art and a science.

The loop is created by using your rod and fly line. When you move the rod to direct the fly line, the line's weight and inertia resist. This resistance causes the rod to bend. The bending of the rod is called loading the rod. When the rod is bent or loaded, it contains potential energy. You will use this energy to propel your fly line allowing your loop to unroll.

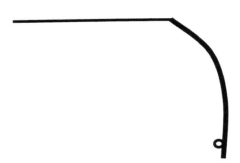 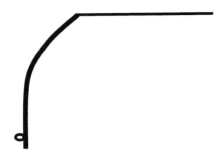

Figure 1- rod bends, loaded for back cast   **Figure 2- rod bends, loaded for forward cast**

When you stop the rod it changes from bent to straight, it unloads. The stored energy from the bent rod is transferred to the fly line and loop, and your cast is made. In the process of unloading, the rod pulls the piece of fly line closest to the rod tip with it as it moves from bent to straight. When the rod is straight, it is unloaded. The energy from the rod springing from bent to straight is imparted to the fly line. The loop is formed and the energy is now in the loop of fly line. This energy allows the loop to continue unrolling your leader and present your fly. This is the action of your rod: it bends and unbends or loads and unloads. This allows you to propel the fly line backward and forward.

The fly rod action has been compared to a spring or lever. You put the lever or spring under tension, direct it where you want it to go, and release. The spring or lever will straighten and propel an object attached to it in the direction of the springing to straight. Think of shooting an elastic. You pull the elastic under tension, aim it at your target then release. The elastic is propelled through the air toward your target. Fly casting is a lot like this. You pull the rod into a bend, and aim it at your target. In order to release the bend you stop the rod. When you stop the rod, it springs to straight and propels your fly line toward your target.

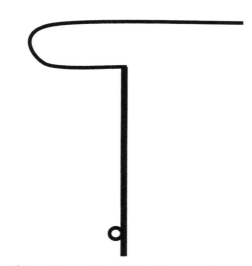

Figure 3- loop forms after rod straightens, unloads

The rod must be under tension for the bending and unbending of the rod to work for you. When you start the cast and move the rod, the line will resist causing the rod to bend. In order to keep the rod bent you need to use acceleration. If you move your hand at a constant rate of speed the rod does not bend, and no loop is formed. This results in your line merely waving back and forth in the air, with no loop to propel your fly. In order to get the rod to bend, you need to accelerate the rod.

The casting stroke starts slowly and then accelerates until the end of the stroke. Acceleration is a change in speed. Therefore, the cast starts slowly and builds speed smoothly and gradually, until the stop. This does not mean to move fast. The artfulness in fly casting is about using just the right amount of speed for each situation.

If you use too much speed as you start the cast, starting like a car speeding away from a red light leaving rubber as it accelerates, you are likely to get a closed loop. A closed loop is called a tailing loop. The tailing loop is caused when the rod tip to moves in a concave path not a straight path. In this case, by accelerating too fast.

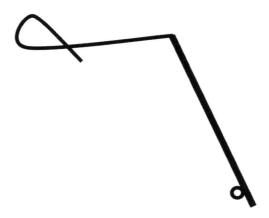

Figure 4- tailing loop

If you do not accelerate and move your hand at a constant speed, you will not get a bend in the rod. When you stop your movement, the rod does not spring to straight and no loop is formed. You must learn to accelerate the rod to a stop. The rod must bend and unbend, and using the weight of the fly line, create open-ended unrolling loops to deliver your fly. You need to get the rod bent, and then pull into that bend by accelerating through the stroke. The stroke ends, finally releasing the bend to propel the line and fly. The cadence of the cast is from slow to fast, accelerating to a stop.

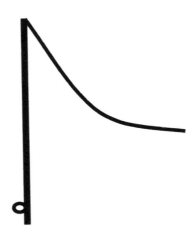

Figure 5- no loop without acceleration

You need a loop on your back cast as well as on your forward cast. Each cast, a back cast and a forward cast are separate entities. What connects them is timing. When the back cast ends, the loop of line is propelled behind you. The forward cast should not start until the back cast loop has unrolled. You must wait for the loop to unroll before starting the forward cast. There is a pause, which connects the two casts. The pause allows time for the loop to unroll.

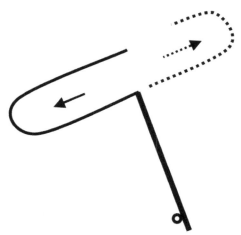

Figure 6- loop on back cast and forward cast

The casting loops are made at an angle. The back cast loop is aimed directly opposite your target and your forward cast is aimed directly toward your target. These two loops are on a straight line (180°) this is your most efficient casting. The straight line is on an angle, an angle directly away from your target on the back cast and directly toward your target on the forward cast.

The angle will change depending on the length of line being cast and the distance to the target. Part of your job is to determine what the perfect angle will be. The closer you are to the target and the shorter the line you are casting, the steeper the angle. As you cast to a more distant target, you will cast a longer line and the angle will be less steep.

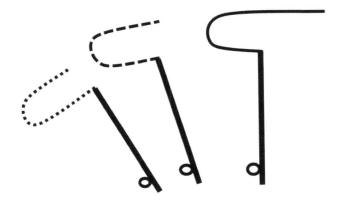

Figure 7- loops are angled to match distance to target: L-R: close, moderate distant target

Summary:

The casting stroke:
- Goal is to form open ended unrolling loops
- Weight is in the fly line
- Loop delivers the fly
- Fly casting system works under tension
- Pull against the weight of the fly line to load the rod
- Rod loading is creating a bent rod
- Unloading is the rod springing back to be straight
- Casting stroke starts slowly and accelerates to a stop
- Loop forms on the stop by the rod springing to straight, taking fly line with it
- Loops for back cast and forward cast are connected by timing
- Straight line casting: back cast loop aimed way from target, forward cast loop is aimed toward target
- Loops have an angle toward or away from the target, which matches the trajectory to reach the target

Equipment

When starting in fly casting you will need to have a basic understanding of how the equipment works. You will also need to understand a few concepts in order to make good selections for your initial fly fishing equipment. There are entire books that discuss the detail of different gear components and their specialty features. I will give you an overview of the equipment, which will serve as a good basis to make your initial equipment choices.

To start in fly fishing your major equipment selections will include the fly rod, reel, fly line and lastly the flies. You will want to match the rod and line to the species of fish you plan to target. The first decision to make is what type of fish you will target for your fly fishing. Next, you need to know something about the environment of that fish. Will you fish in a lake, stream or ocean? Is it generally windy or calm? Do you need to cast far, or is twenty feet sufficient? One rod, reel and fly line outfit will not work perfectly in all situations. Answering these questions will help guide your equipment selections.

Rods

Rods are available in different sizes, lengths, and actions, and are designed for saltwater or freshwater. The rod is your spring or lever, which propels the fly line and fly to the fish. The rod will also help you fight the fish. You need a rod that has sufficient spring to cast the size fly line and flies you will use and enough strength to help you fight the fish. Freshwater rods are used for trout, bass, sunfish etc. These rods are usually 3 to 6 weight (more about this under fly lines) and are designed for freshwater environments. Although you may occasionally use the rod in saltwater, it is not designed to last in the corrosive saltwater environment. Saltwater rods are made with corrosion resistant materials; they have an anodized metal reel seat and larger guides to accommodate larger fly lines.

The size of the rod or line weight of the rod refers to the size fly line and size flies that it is designed to cast. Generally the greater the line weight size, the heftier the rod. While you could catch sunfish on a 9 weight rod, you would feel over powered. If you more closely match your rod to the fish and use a 3 or 5 weight rod, you would get more feeling throughout the experience. Rod sizes range from 2 to 15 weights. The higher numbers are for larger saltwater fish, while the lower rod weights are for freshwater fish, which are generally smaller size.

Rods have action. The spring flex of the rod propels your fly line and fly to the fish. Rod action is usually described as very fast, fast, or medium. This refers to how far from the tip that the rod tends to bend. A very fast action rod will bend about a quarter or less of the rod. A medium action rod may bend to the middle of the rod. Fast actions rods tend to be a stiffer spring. They will give a lot of spring for their small amount of rod bend. These rods are generally suited for saltwater casting where you frequently have to make a long cast and need the rod to be a strong spring. They are also suited to a more aggressive caster who tends to be more forceful in their casting stroke. Slower action rods will bend further down the length of the rod. They generally like a slower tempo to the cast and are well suited to a more patient, relaxed caster. Slower action rods are often used in freshwater situations, or when you do not need to cast particularly large flies or very far. Although these rods can cast distance and deliver large flies, it is more difficult for a beginner to accomplish this. The delicateness of the slower rod is an aspect many casters prefer.

The standard rod length is 9 feet. A short rod (6-7 ft. length) is useful if you are fishing in small mountains streams, or areas with a lot of brush, or you are making very short casts (under 30 ft). Occasionally, a longer rod (10-11 ft.) is preferred if you plan to be casting longer distances while in a canoe of float tube and you are low to the water. To begin fly fishing in freshwater for trout or bass, a 5 or 6 weight rod of 8'6 or 9 ft. is recommended. For saltwater fishing, an 8 or 9 weight rod of 9 ft. length is a great all around rod which can be used for stripers, bluefish, false albacore, bonefish and more.

Reels

Fly reels have two main functions. They hold the fly line and backing, and provide a braking system called drag. The drag keeps your reel from overrunning itself when the fish pulls out fly line, and provides some resistance for the fish as he runs away after being hooked.

Reels are made for freshwater or saltwater. Saltwater reels can hold larger fly lines and more backing (see below). These aspects are important as saltwater fish tend to be larger and run further than the typical trout (salmon and steelhead have the same requirements as saltwater fish). The saltwater reel should be made of corrosion resistant material and the drag mechanism will be larger so it can provide sufficient resistance for the larger fish. Freshwater reels will accommodate an appropriate freshwater sized line and a smaller amount of backing. Most freshwater reels will have lighter drag systems matched to the species of fish you are targeting. When fishing, your drag should be set at 1/3 the breaking strength of the tippet material. You want the drag to become engaged as the fish runs away from you. This is what helps you in the battle of fighting your fish.

Reels can be right or left hand retrieve. This means you can choose to reel with either your right hand or your left hand. Although I am a right handed caster, I prefer to reel with my left hand. When I make a cast with my right hand, I am holding the rod in my right hand and using my left hand to manage my fly line (more about stripping in the section of fighting fish). This allows me to use my stronger right hand to lift the rod and put pressure on the fish. Equally acceptable is to switch the rod to your left hand when you have hooked the fish and are ready to reel the line onto the reel. Right or left hand retrieve is personal preference. Most reels can be switched from right to left hand retrieve or vice versa. Consult your local fly shop for assistance. Remember that most of your time will be casting, not reeling in fish.

When purchasing a reel you need to know what size fly line and amount of backing it can hold. Manufacturers readily publish this information in their brochures and on their websites. Your line and backing requirements are determined by the species you are fishing targeting. A general suggestion is a freshwater reel that accommodates 5 or 6 weight fly line and 100-150 yards of backing. For a saltwater reel, select a reel that accommodates 7-9 weight fly line and 250-275 yards of backing.

Backing

Backing is the material that is placed on your fly reel first. It is a braided Dacron and is very strong for its relative diameter. Saltwater anglers generally use thirty pound strength backing. Freshwater reels are usually set up with twenty pound backing. The backing fills up your fly reel so the line is not in tiny little coils when it comes off the reel. It also extends the range that you can play or fight your fish. A large fish will run a distance that exceeds the length of your fly line. It is common for large fish to run more than one hundred feet away. The backing keeps you connected to the fish and allows you to play the fish at this distance. Without backing, if the fish reaches the end of the fly line and breaks off, you would lose your fly line and the fish.

Fly line

The fly line is the key component of your entire fly fishing system. The fly line is what delivers your fly to the fish. It must be of sufficient weight to handle the size of fly you will be casting. Fly lines at first glance may seem quite simple, but they are not. Every fly line has a design, or taper. The fly line has a thin beginning part called the front taper. This looks somewhat like a sharpened pencil point, which starts narrow and builds to a wider diameter. Next is the belly of the fly line. This is generally the thickest part of the line. After this wider diameter, the line tapers down again (the rear taper) to a thin diameter line. This thin diameter line is called running line. The running line is the line you will use to shoot, when you extend the range of your casting. The front taper, belly and rear taper, are collectively referred to as the head of the fly line. This is the part of the line which has the weight, and the section of the line to use when casting.

The manufacturers have a standard to decide which fly line is which weight. All fly lines are measured by how much they weigh in the first 30 feet of fly line. This measurement is in grains. The amount of grain weight in the first 30 feet determines what size line it is. Therefore, all 5 weight fly lines will weigh the same in the first 30 ft. of line. All 9 weight lines will weigh approximately the same in this first 30 feet. What is likely to differ is the design of the line, any special coatings, or core materials. All of these properties affect how the line will perform in the water and casting. Most fly lines are 90-100 ft. in length. Specialty lines may be shorter or longer. The important focus should be on matching the fly line to the rod. If you have a 5 weight fly rod, use a 5 weight line. A 9 weight rod should have a 9 weight line. The rod companies design the rods to maximize performance with the fly line weight that matches the rod.

Leaders

From the tip of your fly line to your fly is a piece of monofilament called the leader. You cannot make those beautiful fly casting loops without a leader. Energy from your loop of fly line transfers down the monofilament leader, unrolling the loop to present your fly to the fish. Without a leader, your fly line would kick or buck when the loop unrolls and the energy is abruptly dissipated. The leader helps your fly line much like a tail helps stabilize a kite. The leader is also part of your stealth approach to fooling your fish to eat your fly. If you tied your fly directly to your fly line, you would not be subtle in your presentation. Also without a leader, you would change the design of your fly line each time you cut off some your fly line to change your fly. Using a leader preserves the fly line design.

Like your fly line, the leader also has a design. For most situations, your leader should be tapered. That means it will start thickest near the fly line, called the butt section. The leader will gradually get thinner as it tapers down to its end. The mid section of the leader is thinner than the butt section, yet not as thin as the end of your leader. The thinnest section of leader is where your fly will attach. The leader has a butt section, mid section and the thinnest part called tippet. The tapered leader helps smooth the unrolling loop of fly line so your fly is presented gracefully on the water.

You will need to consider leader length. For striper fishing a short leader of 6-8 ft. is sufficient. When fishing in freshwater, or to spooky saltwater fish your leader may need to be 9-15 ft in length. I would suggest starting with 9 ft and adjusting as the fishing requires. If you scare the fish away, you will need to add more tippet material and lengthen the leader. As you spend your day casting and fishing, you are likely to need to tie on more than one fly. Perhaps you loose a fly or you want to change flies because it is not productive. As you cut off one fly and tie on another, you lose a little of your tippet. At some point, your leader is too short for stealth, and the tapered design is affected. You will need to add more tippet material.

Tippet is the monofilament you add to the thinnest section of your leader to provide stealth in your presentation of the fly. Tippet material is purchased on a spool. You add this to the end of your tapered leader. A good general rule is to add more tippet after 8-10 inches of tippet have been lost from your original leader, or if the fish are too spooky. If your fishing is very technical, consult a specialty book for more detailed information on leader construction.

Leaders can be purchased as a manufactured, tapered leader. This is easiest and I recommend this for beginner fly fisherman. The packages of leader will usually tell you the butt diameter, the tippet diameter and how strong it is. Saltwater anglers refer to pounds of test strength to discuss how strong a material is. Ten pound test will break if the force applied exceeds 10 pounds. Freshwater anglers do not talk about pound test strength, rather they use the X system. The X system is an old English system designed to tell how fine or thin a material is. The higher the number of Xs, the thinner the material. To get some idea of how strong a material is, you can use the rule of 10. The rule of 10 refers to subtracting the number of Xs from 10 to get approximate test pound strength of your tippet. For example, 1X tippet is approximately 9 pound test strength (10-1=9) and 6 x tippet is approximately 4 pounds test strength (10-6=4). Remember that 0X is equal to 10 pound strength.

For freshwater start with a tapered leader of 9 feet, which ends in 2X. Carry some spools of tippet for 2x, 4x and 6X. Add sections of tippet material for the length and thinness you need to fish. When you add tippet you want it to be a smooth, gradual thinning of the leader. The step down between sections should be not greater than 2X. For example, 0x to 2x to 4x to 6x, each piece you add will generally be 18-24 inches. For saltwater leaders, start with a 9 foot leader ending in approximately 12-15 pound strength. Carry tippet in spools of 10, 12 or 15 pound test. This is a good place to start.

Flies

There are hundreds if not thousands of different types of flies. This can be overwhelming for the beginner fly fisherman. Hundreds of books have been written about flies and selecting the correct one. I will not try to adequately cover the full range of options available in flies. I will give you the condensed, down and dirty minimalist approach to understanding flies. Flies are generally meant to imitate something that is naturally found in the fish's environment that he would normally desire to eat. There are some exceptions, such as stimulator flies which trigger the fish's natural reaction to eat. Most often, if you select a fly that resembles a normally available food item for the fish, you are more likely to get the fish's interest. Another general concept to understanding flies is that fish feed at different levels of the water. Flies are designed to imitate food found at the different water levels. Flies are designed to be fished on the surface of the water, in the middle for the water depth, or deep, near the bottom of the water depth.

Lastly, you should understand that the fly, is only feathers, yarn, or artificial hair on a hook. It is designed to resemble food items. The fly needs some kind of action to make it look like food. This action can be action within the fly created by the fly's materials, or you may need to impart that action in the form of stripping (see section of fishing). Each type of fly is fished differently. Whether you are using a dry fly in a river or a wet fly in the ocean, you are always concerned with making the fly appear natural for the given environment and enticing to the fish.

The best advice for learning which flies to use in a situation is to ask a local fly shop for advice, fish with a more experienced friend or hire a local guide. Hiring a guide may be more expensive initially but will save you hours of trial and error as you learn from a professional.

Assembling your gear

To put your gear together, start by assembling your rod. Most fly rods are multi piece. They may be two pieces or up to seven pieces, the most common being three or four pieces. They all assemble the same. Start with the thinnest section, the top section and work your way down the rod. The ends of each section have ferrules, which fit together. I recommend that you align the pieces so they are offset by ninety degrees. Slide the male and female pieces together and twist the sections so the guides are aligned. Hold the sections in your hand and look down the middle to see if they appear aligned. If so, continue adding the sections until the rod is complete.

Now add the reel. You should know if your reel is right hand or left hand retrieve. Be sure the reel hand is on the correct side (right or left). Find the cut out in your reel seat (bottom of your rod), insert the foot of the reel into this cut out. Slide the nut up to secure the reel in place then tighten the locking nut. These two rings should be tightened separately for maximum security. You will want your reel to stay secure throughout your day of fishing, but do not want it more than finger tight, as you need to remove it later. Remember in fly casting the reel is on the bottom of the rod and the guides point down.

Strip about fifteen feet of line off your reel, allow this to fall at your feet. Find a clean place to put your reel down where it will not fall, and you will not get dirt inside. Take the front of your fly line and make a loop.

Use this loop and pass it up through each of the guides. When you reach the rod tip, pull out any remaining line and the leader. To be sure you have not missed any guides, hold the leader in your left hand and secure the line and rod in your right hand. Pull the rod into a bend and look, to be sure the line goes through all of the guides. It is easy to miss a guide. If you are practicing and not fishing, be sure to have a yarn fly on your leader to see the leader and fly placement.

Gear Recommendations

	Freshwater	Saltwater
Rod	5 or 6 wt. , 8'6" or 9 ft medium fast to fast action	7-9 wt, 9 foot, fast action
Reel	Accommodate 5-6 wt. line 125 yards of 20 pound backing	Accommodate 7-9 wt line 200-275 yards of 30 pound backing
Fly line	Matching 5 or 6 wt, weight forward, floating line	Matching 7-9 wt. line Weight forward floating line Intermediate fly line if fishing from shore for stripers
Leader	9 ft leader ending in 2x, add sections of tippet for final length and thinness	6-8 ft 12-15 pound for stripers 9ft 10-12 pound for other saltwater fish
Tippet	2x,4x,6x spools	10, 12 and 15 pound spools
Flies	Ask your local fly shop	Ask your local fly shop

Casting Mechanics

Grip

Your choice of grip can help you make the cast by allowing you to maximize your control of the fly rod. Since the fly rod acts like a lever or spring your grip in essence controls that spring. I suggest either thumb or forefinger on top. Both grips allow the rod to be controlled well throughout the cast with little lateral sway.

The thumb on top is the strongest grip for most people. With your thumb on top, the index finger is on the opposite side of the rod butt. You want the thumb and index finger to balance the rod, with your lower three fingers gently wrapped around the rod butt. A key feature of your grip is to be sure the heel of your hand sits on top of the cork grip. Your lower three fingers cradle the rod butt low in the fingers, like when you lift a suitcase handle. The primary points of pressure are your thumb and index finger, and your lower two fingers. Your middle finger is less important for controlling the rod, thus is available to help manage your fly line with shooting and stripping.

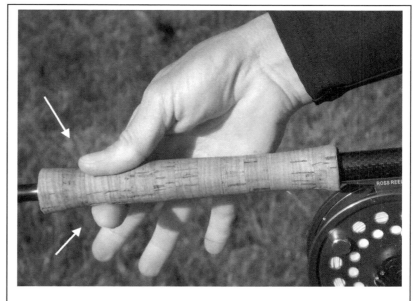

Photo series 1- top: thumb on top, index finger opposite; bottom: line hand traps line, heel of hand sits on top of rod butt

The forefinger on top grip can also be used. This grip also allows the rod butt to be well controlled with minimal sway. The forefinger on top may feel more natural to some people. This grip can be used with accuracy and delicacy by using the index finger to point at the target when you stop the rod. Using this grip, your rod butt should be in line with the underside of your forearm.

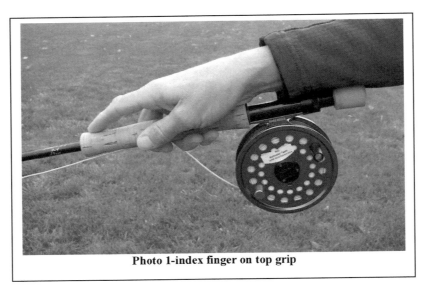

Photo 1-index finger on top grip

Hand tension

Tension in your hand can ruin a day of fishing and is exhausting. Your hand should not squeeze tightly throughout the cast. Rather the hand should hold the rod butt just firmly enough to control the rod. Think about holding the rod butt with the same amount of tension as a raw egg, just enough to control it but not crush it.

Photo 2- relaxed hand to start cast

There is a place for hand tension in your cast. When you stop the rod your hand should tighten, squeezing to a stop. This tension helps stop the movement of the rod. This stop is what gets the energy from the bent rod released into the fly line and creates your loop.

On the back cast, your hand should start relaxed with no tension. As your hand and arm move through the stroke, your hand should be relaxed until you stop the rod. When you stop the rod, your hand tightens, squeezing the rod butt. Hold this tension for a moment then relax. When you relax, you will have no more tension in your hand. With your relaxed hand, hold this position.

Photo series 2- L- tension on back cast stop; R- relax after the stop

On the forward cast, your hand starts with no tension, moving the rod butt in a straight line toward the target. When you are ready to stop the rod, you again tighten your hand. Therefore, your hand should be tense only when the rod is being stopped. The remainder of the time, the hand should be relaxed.

 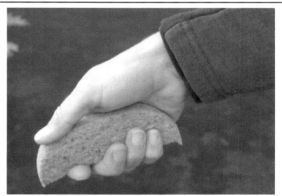

Photo series 3- L- tension on forward cast stop; R- relax after the stop

Arm movement

The hand and arm movement directs the rod and fly line. Your most efficient casting will occur along a straight line, so your rod arm must move in a straight line throughout the casting stroke. In order to create the smooth acceleration and abrupt stop required for the casting stroke, I recommend a method, which uses all the muscles groups and joints of the arm in a compound move.

The forearm moves back and forth toward and away from your body, using your elbow and gives stroke length to the cast. The upper arm lifts and lowers using the shoulder. This incorporates the aiming and trajectory of your cast. The upper arm lifts up on the back cast to help lift your line off the water, and then lowers on the forward cast to aim the fly at the target.

Lastly, use the hand and wrist. The hand will have tension only on the stops and be relaxed yet in control of the rod butt during the casting stroke. The wrist has two positions in the casting stroke. These positions are in relationship of the rod butt to the underside of your forearm. The first position is a bent down position. In this position, the rod butt is parallel with the underside of your forearm and the wrist is in a 0°angle to the rod butt. This is the position of your hand, wrist and forearm to start each back cast. The second position of your wrist is a straight wrist. This creates a 30°- 45° angle from your forearm to the rod butt. This is the wrist position after the stop of the rod on the back cast. Each back cast will start with the rod butt parallel to the forearm and end with the rod butt at a 30°- 45° angle from your forearm. Each forward cast starts with the rod butt at a 45° angle and a straight wrist, and ends with the wrist in the bent down, 0° angle position.

Photo series 4- L- wrist in bent down position; R- wrist in straight position

The compound move of your rod arm is the back and forth motion of your forearm and hand within the up and down motion of your upper arm. These movements need to flow one into the other in a smooth manner. The casting stroke occurs along a diagonal straight line away from and toward your target. To achieve this straight line you need to move your rod arm back and up on the back cast, then down and forward on the forward cast. If you perform these actions as separate moves, it becomes a stair-step motion: first back then up.

You need a straight line for the cast. Think about a staircase. The steps are a series of horizontal then vertical straight lines. If you look at the side of the staircase, you can see a diagonal line that connects this series of horizontal and vertical moves. Your rod arm movements should follow this diagonal straight line. The forearm and upper arm move in a diagonal straight line up behind you for the back cast and along a diagonal straight line down and out for your forward cast. By allowing the arm movements to flow into each other, this accomplishes the diagonal straight lines which good fly casting requires.

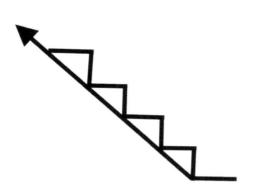

Figure 8- arm movement is coordinated along a straight line

Photo 3-rod arm moves in a straight-line back and up for back cast

In summary, the casting stroke involves the back and forth motion of the forearm and hand, within the up and down motion of the upper arm, within the rotation of the wrist. It is a series of movements to create a diagonal straight line path of the rod.

Wrist action

The wrist can be very helpful to your casting, but must be used in moderation. A little bit of wrist goes a long way. The wrist has two positions, bent down which is 0° angle to your forearm and straight which is a 30-45° angle to you forearm. The change in positions helps to stop and unload the rod.

Every back casts starts with your wrist in the bent down position and ends with your wrist in the straight position, and the rod butt approximately 45° to your forearm. This change of angle occurs when you squeeze the rod to affect the stop and then relax. When you firmly squeeze the rod butt, hold this position for a moment. Then relax your grip and the rod butt will automatically be repositioned. The rod butt is now 45° from the underside of your forearm. It is the structure of your hand and slight rotation of the wrist, which accomplishes this change in angle.

Photo 4-start back cast, wrist in bent down position, rod butt is 0 degree angle

Photo 5-end back cast, wrist in straight position, rod butt at 45 degree angle

The forward cast starts with the wrist in the straight position, a 30-45°angle of the rod butt to your forearm, and ends with your wrist in the bent down, 0° position. On the forward cast, the wrist rotation is enacted differently. You can now use your natural muscle coordination in a forward direction and rotate your wrist forward on the stop. When making the forward cast, start with the wrist straight position and move your rod arm toward your target.

Photo 7- forward cast starts with straight wrist

Photo 6-- thumb pushes, lower fingers pull back

When you are ready to stop, push forward with your thumb on the rod butt handle, while simultaneously pulling back with your lower fingers. This causes your wrist to rotate and return to the bent down position, closing that 45° angle to a 0° angle. This pushing pulling motion stops the rod abruptly for proper unloading of the rod and transferring energy for the cast. This action of the hand and wrist to open and close the rod butt angle is what Joan Wulff calls a power snap.

Photo 8- forward cast ends with bent down wrist

The wrist rotation occurs while your rod arm moves within the casting stroke. The wrist rotation starts when the thumb pad is 90 ° to, or directly opposite the target. It ends with the thumb aimed 45° to the target. The wrist rotation occurs over a few inches. It is not a stop in place but occurs over a small amount of distance within the casting stroke. When the wrist rotation is complete, the rod is stopped and the casting stroke has ended.

To summarize, the wrist has two positions, bent down and straight. The corresponding angles of the rod butt to forearm are 0° angle for bent down position, and 30°-45° angle for the straight wrist position. Every back cast starts with the wrist in the bent down position and ends with the wrist in the straight position (the wrist angle changes from 0° to 30-45°). Each forward cast starts with the wrist in the straight position and ends with the wrist in the bent down position (the wrist angle changes from a 30-45°angle to 0°).

Rod Arm Mechanics

Arm part	Joint	Action
Hand	Wrist	Holds the rod and stops the rod with tension Wrist positions: Bent down (0°) and straight (45°)
Forearm	Elbow	Moves back and forth to give stroke length
Upper arm	Shoulder	Lifts and lowers to facilitate trajectory and aiming the cast

Rod Arm Movement Sequence

	Back cast	Forward cast
Loading the rod	1) Starts lifting line with the forearm and hand 2) Continues with upper arm, see elbow lift! 3) Trajectory of lift ↗	1) Starts with upper arm lowering from the shoulder, see elbow lower! 2) Continues with forearm extending slightly to line up thumb with target 3) Trajectory toward your target ↙
Unloading the rod	Hand Squeezes to a stop then relaxes, Wrist rotates to straight Rod butt at 30-45° angle to forearm	Hand tightens: Push with thumb, pull back with lower fingers Wrist rotates to bent down Rod butt now parallel with forearm (0° angle)
Follow through	After the cast rod tip may drift to a new position- an optional move	After the cast the rod tip is lowered to the water

Each cast must first get the line, leader, and fly under tension and moving as a unit. Then bend the rod under this tension. The hand motion is always at the end of the cast. Hand tension stops the rod to trigger the unloading of the rod and loop formation.

Casting Concepts

Fly casting has a number of concepts which are used to describe the nature of the cast. These concepts are critical to your understanding of what the fly cast is about and how to make a good cast. These concepts are interrelated and flow together to create a beautiful cast. The fly cast occurs in a relatively short time and it is difficult to see each of the components of the cast. Therefore, a detailed discussion of the casting terms and concepts is presented here for your review both as a novice, and as you progress in your casting. Remember the concepts build together to create the perfect cast.

Casting Stroke

The casting stroke is the path of your rod and hand during the cast. The casting stroke is the back and forth motion of your forearm and hand while you move the rod from a start to a stop position. The casting stroke is about bending or loading the rod. The stroke length must be matched to the amount of bend in the rod and the length of line being cast. There is a phrase to convey this concept: short cast-short stroke, long cast-long stroke. In short casts your rod moves a short amount because you need a small amount of rod loading. In longer casts, you need more loading of the rod so the casting stroke lengthens.

The nature of the casting stroke and its acceleration is one of the more difficult concepts to learn. The casting stroke starts slowly and accelerates to a stop. This means there is a change in speed. The cast smoothly accelerates, going a little faster as you move through the casting stroke and ends abruptly. The acceleration within your casting stroke is crucial to make a good cast. Much like Goldilocks, you need it to be "just right". Not enough acceleration and the cast will not fully develop or reach its potential. Too much speed and the cast suffers from the excess energy that must be dissipated. This usually results in a negative impact on your cast.

Loading and Unloading the rod

The fundamental principles in making any cast are the loading and unloading of the fly rod. You need to first bend the rod and then allow it to unbend. This transfers the energy to the fly line to propel your loop and fly to your target. Without a bend and unbend, no cast is created. The loading and unloading of the rod truly is the focal point of fly casting and many of the problems in fly casting are related to the ability to properly load and unload the fly rod.

When you start the casting stroke and move the rod in a direction for your cast, the rod will bend against the weight and resistance of the fly line. As the rod begins to bend, you need to accelerate the rod to maintain or deepen the bend in the rod. If you move the rod at a constant speed, the rod will not bend. You must accelerate the rod to bend the rod. For a short cast you are propelling a short line and less weight, so a small bend or load in the rod is sufficient.

If you are casting a longer line with more weight, or want to shoot line, you will need more load in the rod. In order to get a deeper load in the rod you will need a longer casting stroke, you need to accelerate over a longer distance to get that deeper bend.

The loading is about getting the rod, fly line, leader, and fly under tension and creating a bend in the rod. Then position this system under tension in a direction you want the fly line to travel after you stop the rod. The movement of your rod arm through the casting stroke to create the bend is called a loading move. Translational movement is the newer term used to describe the lateral movement of the rod as you accelerate in the casting stroke.

After the rod is loaded, you will want to harness that potential energy and use it to make your cast. Your goal is to efficiently unload the rod transferring the energy from the bent rod to the fly line. The more efficiently you stop the rod, the more energy you can transfer to the fly line and the more you are using your rod to make the cast with less physical demands on you and your casting arm!

Stopping the rod is not a natural motion. This is again, where fly casting is unique. To unload the rod the casting stroke needs to come to an abrupt and complete stop. Lefty Kreh refers to this part of the casting stroke as the speed up and stop. The stop triggers the rod's action of moving from bent to straight and the casting loop forms. To help you stop the rod you will use a slight wrist rotation on both the back cast and forward cast. The wrist rotation is a small movement. It is not about being powerful. It is more about the timing and quickness of the wrist rotation. This wrist rotation completes the acceleration of the cast (getting the rod loaded) and stops the rod. When the rod stops, the rod flips to straight and the loop forms. Joan Wulff has described this wrist rotation as a power snap. Another term recently used is a rotational movement. These terms describe the wrist rotation, which occurs at the end of the casting stroke.

Follow Through and Drift

After the forward casting stroke has ended the rod tip may be repositioned from the stop point. This is called follow through. Typically, the rod is positioned down toward the water to help settle the cast and be ready for fishing. Follow through occurs without power and is a relaxed move. Drift is an advanced technique, which repositions the rod after the back cast stop. Both follow through and drift occur after the stop, they are optional movements and are separate from the casting stroke.

Timing

Timing refers to the pause between each cast, both the back cast and the forward cast. Perfect timing allows the loop to unroll completely, but not fall or loose altitude before you start the next cast. The loop just unrolls but the line is still under tension. If you hear a bullwhip or cracking sound when you cast, you have been too quick. Slow down and wait a little longer before starting your next cast. If you wait too long, the line will fall, and you lose tension on the rod. On the forward cast, you can see your loop unroll, so when false casting it is easy to know when to start the next back cast. Start the next cast when the line has almost unrolled and your loop now resembles the hook of the letter J. You need to anticipate the line being fully unrolled. This visual cue of the letter J will help you recognize when to start the next cast.

On the back cast, everything is behind you and you cannot see the loop. To help you achieve good timing, use your sense of feel. When you stop the rod on your back cast, squeeze your hand for a moment then relax. With a relaxed hand, you can feel the rod bounce or recoil in your hand. When these movements of the rod butt stop, it is time to start your forward cast. You need a soft hand to feel this timing in the rod butt. A good general rule is that a short cast has a short pause and a longer cast has a longer pause.

Casting arc

The casting stroke moves your rod from a start position to a stop position. These positions of your rod are called the casting arc. The casting arc refers to the angles of the rod butt at the start and stop positions of each cast. The two positions form an arc. It is like the capital letter V, with a wider base. The arc must be the appropriate width to accommodate the bend or load in the rod. A short cast needs a narrow arc, and a longer cast requires a wider arc. The size of casting arc must be matched to the amount of bend in the rod. The short cast has less rod bend, so a narrow arc is fine. The longer cast will have more bend in the rod, and a wider arc is needed to maintain a straight line path of the rod tip. The casting arc should also have an angle that matches the cast. For short casts the casting arc is angled downward, a steeper angle. On a longer cast, the arc is angled more toward the horizon, with a less steep angle. To match the casting arc, the phrase to remember is short cast-short stroke-narrow arc, long cast-long stroke and wider arc.

Aiming

You always need to aim your cast, or you have no control over the placement of your fly. Aim the back cast opposite your target and aim the forward cast toward your target. This is on a straight line within the 180° parameters. You can use your thumb to help aim your cast. When learning to fly cast and standing in the closed or vertical stance. Think of aiming your back cast up and back behind you. Keep your forearm in line with your upper arm, and lift your elbow on the back cast. Your cast will be perfectly aimed, up and back behind you, 180 ° opposite your forward target. In this position, you are using your body structure to help aim the cast. At the completion of your back cast, your thumb will be relatively straight upright. Imagine a straight line coming from your thumbnail, directed behind you. This imaginary line should be angled upward or at the horizon, never below the horizon.

On the forward cast, your eyes help guide your aiming. First, look at your target to determine a straight line from your eye to the target. Next, move your rod hand on a diagonal straight line toward your target. Use your thumb to aim your cast. On the forward cast, use your thumb pad. When your thumb pad is aligned directly opposite, or 90° to your target, begin the wrist rotation to stop the rod and aim your loop. Casting within the 180° straight line parameters and using your thumb as reference will help you be more accurate.

Trajectory

When aiming the cast to the target you need to consider if the cast is aimed correctly from right to left (horizontal perspective) and, if the angle of the cast is correct. If the cast unrolls just above the water and flutters down to your target, it is great. If the cast unrolls well above your target and the wind blows it off course, you will need a steeper trajectory. You will want to angle your cast somewhat lower so it unrolls just above your target. If your cast piles up on the water before completely unrolling, your trajectory is too steep. In this case, you ran out of altitude, your cast did not have enough room to unroll. The cast should unroll nicely if you use a shallower angle. The correct trajectory involves adjusting the angle of the casting arc. This judgment comes with experience as you evaluate each cast.

Casting plane

Fly casting can occur at any angle from horizontal on the right to horizontal on the left. The angle of the cast is the casting plane. The casting plane is generally the same angle for the back cast and forward cast. The plane may be adjusted for a particular fishing situation. An accomplished caster will be capable of casting in all casting planes.

Stance

In fly casting, how you stand in relation to your target is called your stance. It refers to the position of your feet, body and rod arm. There are three stances which will cover most of your fishing needs: closed or vertical; off vertical (also called open); and off shoulder. Each stance has its benefits and the correct stance can help you make the cast.

I recommend starting with the closed or vertical stance for the beginner. This is the stance to use when you are trying to solve casting problems. The closed stance involves standing with your feet even, about shoulder width apart and your shoulders faced square to the target. Your rod arm will move in line with your body and shoulders. This stance facilitates moving your rod arm in line with your body helping to make straight lines throughout the casting stroke, and is your strongest position for accuracy.

The off vertical or open stance is favored by many saltwater fishermen or when you need to make longer casts. This stance involves standing with your rod hand side foot dropped back and outward for a wider base. Your hips and shoulder are rotated so they are at a slight angle to the target. You will tilt your forearm away from your body just slightly, but your elbow remains fairly close to your side. This works well for longer casts when you need longer casting strokes, or when standing on a boat and need improved balance.

The final stance is the off shoulder position. This can help you in many fishing situations. If you have wind coming from your casting side, or an obstacle that precludes placing your cast on your dominant casting side. For a right-handed caster, drop back the left foot, and turn your body slightly so the left hip and shoulder is back. Tilt your rod arm slightly to the left. Your elbow will come away from your side as your forearm and hand tilt downward. Remember to keep your rod hand in front of your face to facilitate accuracy. This position allows you to cast on your off shoulder keeping your fly line away from wind and obstacles. You will use this when casting with the rod in your right hand but positioned over your left shoulder.

Tailing loops

Tailing loops are closed loops. They occur when the rod tip moves in a concave path rather than a straight path. Somewhere in the stroke, the rod tip dipped down then flexed up crossing the line. This causes the unrolling line to fall below the bottom leg of the loop closing the loop. This causes knots in the fly line and leader, and ruins the cast. There are many ways to cause this concave path of the rod tip. The most common include abruptly applying power, using too short of a casting stroke and using too narrow of a casting arc for the amount of rod bend.

The Casts

To start in fly casting, I recommend you begin using only one hand. Use the hand you will hold the rod with, this is your rod arm. This allows you to focus on the mechanics of the cast of your rod arm and minimize the variable of your line hand performance. To be operational as a fly fisherman, you must learn two casts: the roll cast and basic cast, and two techniques: false casting and shooting line. This is the minimum skill set needed to be functional in a fishing situation. When casting with just your rod arm, you need to hold the line "trapped" under your middle finger. This will keep the line under tension throughout the casting stroke. Later, when you learn the techniques of false casting and shooting line, you will add your second hand, your line hand. The casting sequences describe the positions for a right hand dominant caster. Those who are left hand dominant should make the appropriate adjustments. The casts use the vertical or closed stance position, unless otherwise noted.

Photo 9-closed stance, vertical position

Before you start to cast, you will need to get some fly line out of the rod tip. After you have strung up the rod, pull approximately 30 ft of fly line off the reel. Let this fall at your feet. Place your leader and tip of fly line in the water. Holding the line loosely in your line hand, wiggle your rod back and forth sideways. This will use the action of your rod and the weight of the line on the water to pull the additional fly line out of the rod tip. When you are finished, you should have a pile of line on the water ready to learn the roll cast.

Roll Cast

The roll cast is the first cast I teach because it allows you to get started fishing immediately. The cast is comprised of only a single forward cast so it is less complex to learn. The roll cast has a set up phase, followed by the forward casting stroke. You have more time to think about the forward cast before starting it. All of these factors make the roll cast the perfect place to start. After you learn the details of the forward cast, you will add the back cast for the basic cast.

The roll cast is traditionally used in situations where you have limited space for a back cast due to obstacles, and there is not enough room for a fully extended back cast. You can also use the roll cast to straighten your line. This is helpful when you first put line on the water, or if you make a mistake and need to straighten your line so you can start the cast over. The roll cast and its variations can be used in many fishing situations, which you will learn as you progress.

The roll cast involves a set up phase then the forward cast. Begin with your proper grip, using the thumb or index finger on top. Use no hand tension and trap the line under your middle finger. Stand with your feet, shoulders and hips facing your target (closed stance). If more comfortable, you may stand with the foot on your dominant side dropped back slightly.

Photo 10-- beginning stance

To make the roll cast you will use a four step method.

1) Lift the line and tilt the rod out from your body at a slight angle.

Keep your elbow close to your body and pivot your forearm and hand to tilt slightly outward. Bring the rod and line back toward your body. Allow the line to fall behind the rod tip creating a D shaped loop. Think of creating the capital letter D with the loop of line behind the rod tip resembling the large curved part of the letter D.

2) Stop and check.

It is important to stop, as you need to allow the line to settle on the water and behind you. Proceed through a series of checkpoints to be sure you are positioned for a good cast. Start with the line on the water. Then work back toward your rod hand and arm. Check that you have line both on the water and bellied behind you for the D loop. From the rod tip, bring your eyes to your rod hand and arm. Check your hand height. It should be at the level of your temple and your hand should be soft, no tension. Check the angle of your rod butt in relation to your forearm. This should be no greater than a 45°angle. Be sure

Roll Cast D Loop

Photo 11-roll cast set up

your rod hand and forearm are tilted slightly away from your body. This ensures the line will not hit you as it comes forward.

3) Aim the cast.

Select a precise target and be sure your elbow is in line with and points at the target. Your primary aiming will be with your thumb pad. However, with your rod hand near your temple, you cannot see your thumb. Your elbow is visible, and is along the same target line as your thumb, just on the opposite side of your arm. Use your elbow to begin aiming. Envision a straight line trajectory toward your target. Be sure your elbow points at your target. Remember to aim the cast to the left of your fly line. If you select a target to the right of the line, the line will cross itself and tangle. From the right hand position, you must cast to the left of your fly line as it sits in the water.

Take your time with the set up. There is no need to rush. A good set up will help you make a better forward cast.

4) Forward cast.

Your elbow is aligned with your target for aiming. The casting stroke starts slowly and accelerates along a straight line to aim your loop toward the target. Because your rod hand is up and the cast must be aimed at an angle down toward the water, when you start the forward casting stroke your elbow will be the first body part to move. Your wrist and forearm maintain their position. They are static during this part of the casting stroke. Your elbow lowers as you line up your thumb pad with your target. You must lower the elbow in order to accelerate your rod on a diagonal line straight toward your target.

Photo series 5- L- roll cast set up; R- start forward stroke

The rod arm sequence of movements is to start with the elbow and finish with your hand. The forward cast movements flow from upper arm to forearm then hand. The upper arm lowers through a shoulder rotation, which allows the elbow to lower. Focus on lowering the elbow. The forearm lowers and extends slightly, to facilitate the diagonal straight line toward the target. Focus on aiming with your thumb pad. Lastly, the hand and wrist are engaged to stop the rod. The primary loading of the rod is from the upper arm and forearm movement. This occurs with acceleration. Start your acceleration slowly. Continue building speed until your thumb is positioned directly opposite your target (90° to the target). If you keep your elbow in place, it is called "hinging" and you cannot move the rod in a straight line if you hinge. Be sure to start the cast by lowering the elbow.

With your thumb lined up 90° to your target, start the wrist rotation to stop the rod and create the loop. Push forward on the cork handle with your thumb, while also pulling back with your lower three fingers. This causes the rod butt and wrist to rotate. Your wrist is now in the bent down or 0° position. The rod butt is in line with your forearm. You have completed the forward cast, congratulations!

Photo series 6- L-stop, wrist bent down; R-follow through to water

After you stop the rod, look for the loop. Watch the loop. It should fire off the tip of the rod and look somewhat like a sideways V, or oval shape. You are looking for this roll cast shape. This V shape will have a point or nose to the loop, not a rounded front. The pointed shape of the sideways V is aerodynamic. It cuts into the wind better and directs more energy of the cast toward the target. This helps the loop fully unroll presenting your fly on target. If you have a rounded front of your loop, the energy is dispersed over a wide area, and is less efficient. With any wind, it may not fully unroll, and you will miss your target. After you have stopped the rod, watch the loop unroll. Slowly lower, your rod tip to the surface of the water, this is called follow through. Follow through helps settle the cast and keeps you in contact with your line, and fly.

This is the roll cast. It is the forward casting stroke. Before moving on, practice the roll cast following the four step approach and watching the shape of the loop. As you are learning, remember to be aware of hand tension. When you start the forward cast, your hand should have no tension. When you make the wrist rotation, you do have hand tension. During follow thorough, your hand relaxes and no longer has tension. Remember the casting stroke sequence: upper arm, forearm and hand. Leading with the elbow and finishing with the hand and wrist.

When you have practiced roll casting on your dominant shoulder it is time to learn the roll cast on the non-dominant side casting side or off shoulder stance. Casting on your right side, you aimed your cast to your left. When fishing, you must be able to cast to both sides. The off shoulder position allows you to cast toward the right. You will use the off shoulder position if the wind is blowing on your dominant side causing the line to blow into your body. If the target fish is on your right, or if the line on the water is on your left side, and you need to cast toward the right side, and will use the off shoulder roll cast.

The off shoulder stance involves switching your feet so the line side foot will drop back slightly. Your shoulders and hips will turn slightly to your left. Next, allow your elbow to come away from your side as you tip your forearm and palm inward, in front of your face. The wrist and forearm are still in alignment, just at an angle in, toward your body rather than away from your body.

Photo 12- off shoulder stance

Follow the four steps of the roll cast:
1) Lift and tilt.
    Draw the line back toward you so the loop of line falls behind your non-dominant side to create the D loop.
2) Stop and check.
    Be sure to allow the line to settle on the water and behind you. Start with the line on the water and work back toward your rod hand and arm. Check that you have line both on the water and bellied behind you for the D loop. Check your hand height. It should be at the level of your temple. Your hand should have no tension. Check the angle of your rod butt in relation to your forearm. It should be approximately a 45° angle. Be sure your rod hand and forearm are aligned. The elbow is out away from your body, while your hand is in front of your face.
3) Aim your cast.
    Be sure your elbow is pointed at your target.

Photo series 7- L- off shoulder set up; R- rod angled over left of body

4) Forward cast.

Start the forward casting stroke by lowering your elbow as you line up your thumb pad with the target. Your wrist and forearm maintain their position during this part of the casting stroke. The rod arm sequence of movements remains the same. Start with the elbow and finish with your hand. The movements flow from upper arm to forearm then hand. When your thumb is opposite the target, start the wrist rotation to stop the rod. Push forward on the cork handle with your thumb, while also pulling back with your lower three fingers. Watch your loop unroll and follow through with the rod tip down to the water.

Photo series 8- L- off shoulder stop; R- off shoulder follow through

The wind, your line placement and the fish's location will determine whether to use the dominant or non-dominant side for your cast. With the D loop on your right, you must cast to a target on your left. With your D loop on your left, you must cast to a target on your right. This will allow the line to unroll without crossing itself. Remember to change your stance and tilt the elbow (in or out) to facilitate the placement of the D loop in the correct position to make the cast. Practice the roll cast on both the dominant and non-dominant sides so you will be ready for any fishing conditions.

Rod arm movement sequence

	Forward cast
Loading the rod	4) Starts with upper arm lowering from the shoulder, see elbow lower! 5) Continues with forearm extending slightly to line up thumb with target 6) Trajectory toward your target
Unloading the rod	Hand tightens: Push with thumb, pull back with lower fingers Wrist rotates to bent down Rod butt now parallel with forearm (0° angle)
Follow through	After the cast the rod tip is lowered to the water

Roll Cast:
1) Lift & tilt rod
2) Position to a stop & check
3) Aim cast
4) Forward cast

Basic Cast

The basic cast is the classic fly cast. It has both a back cast and a forward cast. Each cast is separate. The two casts are connected through timing. You already know the forward cast so now you must build a back cast. The back cast stroke involves the same concepts as the forward cast. The back cast is an overall acceleration to a stop that requires the loading and unloading of the fly rod to create the loop. This cast must be aimed along a straight line up and behind you.

Stand in the vertical stance with your feet, shoulders and hips facing your target. The rod cannot bend until the line is under tension. Use the roll cast to straighten the line and remove slack. Starting with the line straight on the water, use your rod hand and forearm as a unit to lift the line off the water. Lift with your wrist in the bent down position, using your forearm and hand. Your hand has no tension.

Photo 13- back cast start position

Remember that all casts start slowly and build their acceleration gradually. Lift the line off the water with just enough speed so you lift it inch by inch. Watch the line in front of you to know the correct speed for your lift. If you lift too fast, you will see the water spray as it rips off the water surface. This tells every fish around that you are there and is not subtle at all. If you lift too slowly, you will run out of stroke length. Your forearm will have moved its maximum length and run into your upper arm yet you will not have lifted the line off the water. This typically results in a jerky motion, pulling the fly, endangering you and disturbing the water. The correct speed is determined by watching your line and lifting inch by inch. You should see a small V-shaped wake as you lift the line. This wake shows you have the correct speed.

Photo 14-wrist in bent down position

The path of your hand and forearm is in line with your shoulder and upper arm. This is a diagonal straight line to position your back cast up and behind you, directly opposite where your fly started on the water. How far your hand and forearm move for the casting stroke is determined by the amount of line you need to lift. Your maximum stroke length is when your forearm meets your upper arm. When making a back cast you have a visual cue to use. You will lift until you reach the line-leader connection. This is where the end of your fly line attaches to the monofilament leader. Watch your line lift from the water. When you reach the line leader connection, tighten your grip on the rod butt, and squeeze the rod to a stop!

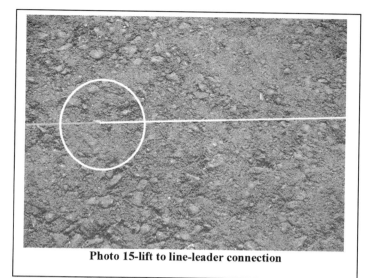
Photo 15-lift to line-leader connection

Your cast has now ended. Hold the stop for a moment then relax your hand. Watch for the rod butt to jump away from your forearm. You will have a 45° angle from your rod butt to your forearm. This position should look familiar. It is the starting position for your forward cast that you learned through the roll cast.

Photo 16- back cast stop

Photo 17-straight wrist, 30-45 degree angle

Now you must focus on timing. Timing is the pause after the cast while the loop unrolls. Perfect timing allows the loop to unroll, but maintains the line under tension. Remember that the cast must bend and unbend the rod, this can only happen when the line is under tension.

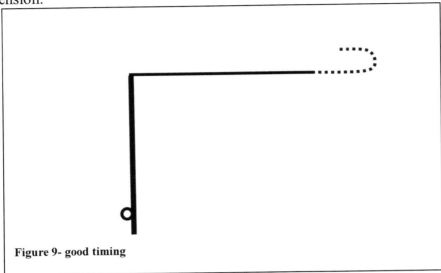

Figure 9- good timing

If your pause is too long, the line will fall to the ground and loose tension, creating slack line. If your pause is too brief, and you start your forward cast too soon, you will have some line unrolling behind while other line starts forward. The line moving in two directions inhibits the smooth acceleration which is critical the loading and unloading of the rod. You will likely hear a cracking sound like a whip and will lose your fly as it snaps off.

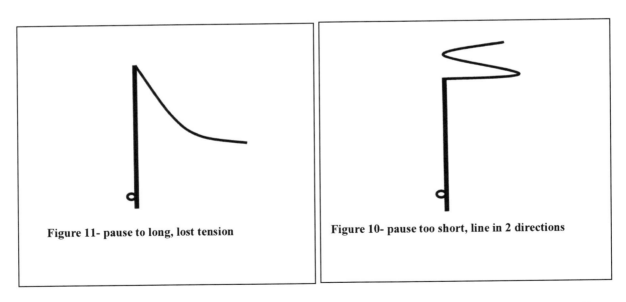

Figure 11- pause to long, lost tension   **Figure 10- pause too short, line in 2 directions**

After the stop when you relax your grip, if you have a soft hand you can feel the line unroll off your rod tip. Watch your rod butt and you will see a shake or recoil in the butt as the cast unrolls. If you have a relaxed hand, you will feel the rod butt recoil. When this

48

movement has stopped, your loop has unrolled and it is time to start your forward cast. Remember that you need to have a soft hand to feel this movement in the rod butt.

Proper timing is a thing of feeling. It will develop with your experience. When first starting in fly casting it can be difficult to remember to relax and be able to get the feel of the cast unrolling. To develop your timing, watch and count the how long it takes the forward cast to unroll. Wait this same amount of time for the back cast to unroll. This is not a perfect system because each length of line and each wind condition will require a different timing. Your timing will also change as you shoot line and lengthen the cast. However, if you have trouble with timing, the counting of the forward cast can help you for a fixed amount of line and a given set of wind conditions. As you progress, I encourage you to work on your feeling. This will allow you to make the needed adjustments while casting.

When your back cast has unrolled, it is time for the forward cast. Do not rush your forward cast. All casts need to start slowly building speed gradually while moving toward the target. Before starting your forward cast, look to your target and think of aiming the cast. Now you can start the rod arm movement in a forward direction to line up your thumb pad with the target. This forward cast does not take as much acceleration as the forward cast of the roll cast. With the roll cast, the line is static and you need to get it under tension and moving from a dead stop. After the back cast the line is in the air, and it takes comparatively less energy and speed to redirect the line in the forward direction.

The path of the forward cast will be at an angle downward to the target area in front of you. Start by lowering your elbow and focus on using your thumb pad to aim. With the line under tension, the rod loaded, and your thumb pad opposite the target area, you are ready for your forward cast wrist rotation. Push forward with your thumb and pull back with your lower fingers. Watch your loop unroll and follow through with the rod tip down to the water.

Photo series 9- L- forward cast stop position; R- follow through to water

If you have a longer line to lift off the water, you will need a longer stroke length. To get this longer stroke on the back cast you can lean forward at the waist, before you start to lift the line. This increases your stroke length with body movement. Your stop position is still not beyond your shoulders. The extra stroke length comes from in front of you by using your body movement.

After you have added body movement, if you need more help to lift the line for your back cast, you can add speed. Use a higher rate of acceleration for longer lines. Do not use so much speed that you disturb the water. Add just a little extra speed so you can lift the longer line.

Now you have a back cast and a forward cast, this is your basic cast. This is the cast, which everyone pictures when they think of a fly cast. Once you have the back cast you can add the techniques of false casting and shooting line.

Basic Cast:
- Lift to the line-leader connection
- Look for spray of water to judge speed of lift
- Stop as fly leaves the water
- Loading move is long
- Wrist rotation on stop is brief
- Timing allows loop to almost unroll
- Forward cast aimed to target

Rod Arm movement sequence

	Back cast	Forward cast
Loading the rod	1) Starts with lifting line with the forearm and hand 2) Continues with upper arm, see elbow lift! 3) Trajectory of lift	1) Starts with upper arm lowering from the shoulder, see elbow lower! 2) Continues with forearm extending slightly to line up thumb with target 3) Trajectory toward your target
Unloading the rod	Hand squeezes to a stop then relaxes Wrist rotates to straight Rod butt at 30-45° angle to forearm	Hand tightens: Push with thumb, pull back with lower fingers Wrist rotates to bent down Rod butt now parallel with forearm (0° angle)
Follow through	After the cast rod tip may drift to a new position- **an optional move**	After the cast the rod tip is lowered to the water

False Casting

Making a series of back casts and forward casts, without letting the line touch the water, is false casting. False casting is used to dry your dry fly. Dry flies are designed to sit on top of the water, but can become waterlogged as you fish. False casting will shake water off the fly and dry it, allowing it to sit on the surface of the water again. You can false cast to change directions, such as from a downstream position to an upstream. It is also used for accuracy. You can measure the cast to see if you have enough line out and are lined up to accurately hit your target.

Photo 18- false cast start position, line secured in left hand

When false casting, you add your line hand. Your line hand's primary responsibility is to maintain tension between the first guide of your rod (stripping guide) and your line hand. The fly line loop can only form if the line is kept under tension. Therefore, the line hand has a very important job.

To begin, your line hand takes the line from your rod hand, which was trapping the line as you cast with one hand. There should be some space between your rod hand and your line hand. This space helps you to keep the line from tangling on your reel as you false cast. As you are learning, you can keep each hand on its respective side of the body. This way you are less likely to move your arms in a swinging club like manner. Unlike baseball or golf where both hands move to one side of the body and perform a swinging motion, the fly casting motion is a straight line motion. Keeping the line hand from crossing the midline of your body will help prevent this swinging motion.

Because the line hand must maintain tension on the line that is between your rod hand and the first stripping guide, you need to watch this piece of fly line. Be sure it is always under tension while casting. In order to keep this line under tension, your line hand must move in unison with your rod hand. When your rod hand lifts and lowers, your line hand also lifts and lowers, creating a mirror image. The line hand moves in a parallel motion. It is a little apart from your rod hand, but in a matching motion to keep the line under tension.

The trajectory changes when false casting. The back cast is still upward and back, but the forward cast trajectory is no longer downward. Since you do not place the fly on the water, the forward cast trajectory is more out, toward the horizon or several feet above your target. The forward cast trajectory is a shallower angle. After false casting, you are ready to present your fly. The presentation cast places the fly on the water and the fly is "presented" to the fish. Make your final forward cast on a downward trajectory to land your fly just above the water.

When false casting you need to be aware of timing. Timing refers to the pause between each cast backward or forward. If your timing is too slow, the line will fall. You will lose tension on your rod and it ruins the cast. You may hear or see you fly hit the water in front of you, or the ground behind you. If you are too fast, you will hear a whip cracking sound and will probably lose a fly. The timing needs to be "just right". With perfect timing, the loop unrolls and the line is kept aloft. There is no sagging of the line and no cracking noises. You can listen to your line to be sure you are not too fast.

Photo series 10- top- line hand maintains tension on line; bottom- false cast stop position

Remember from the basic cast that you can learn to feel the timing by relaxing your rod hand grip after each stop. When you relax your grip, you can feel the rod stop moving in your hand. This signals the rod has unloaded. With a soft hand, you can feel the weight of the line increasing as it unrolls off the rod tip. When the cast has completed unrolling, you can start a cast in the next direction. As you false cast, your hand is squeezing on the stops, and relaxing when the cast unrolls. While developing the feeling, you can use a visual cue on your forward cast. You start the next cast when the loop has almost unrolled and your loop now resembles the hook of the letter J. You need to anticipate the line fully unrolling and start the next cast before it completely unrolls. There will be a delay from when you see the line unrolled and when your body moves for the next cast. To avoid the delay that causes you to lose line tension, you need to anticipate the cast unrolling. This visual cue of the letter J will help you anticipate the line being fully unrolled. This is the cue to start the next cast.

Timing is a variable. The more line you are casting the longer the time it takes for the cast to unroll. A longer line needs a longer pause between back cast and forward cast, it needs slower timing. The loop from a shorter line will take less time to unroll so it needs quicker timing and a shorter pause.

False casting is great for evaluating and adjusting your loop shape. Rod tip path determines the loop shape. Be aware of your casting arc. This is the angle of the rod butt at the stop positions. The arc creates a letter **V**. The way to know you have the correct casting arc is to watch your loops. If the loop is oval shaped then you have a good casting arc. If your arc is too wide, you will have big, open loops. If your arc is too narrow, you will get a tailing loop. A tailing loop is a closed loop, which tangles on itself. A tailing loop can tie knots in your leader and weaken it. Longer lines require a wider casting arc and shorter lengths of line require a narrower casting arc. The trajectory for a narrow arc and short line is steep. Trajectory for a wider arc is shallower. Being able to control the size of your loop is important as your fishing needs will vary.

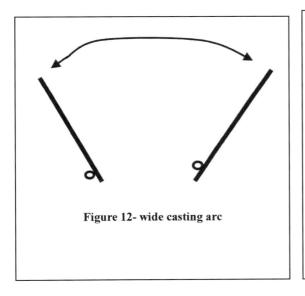

Figure 12- wide casting arc

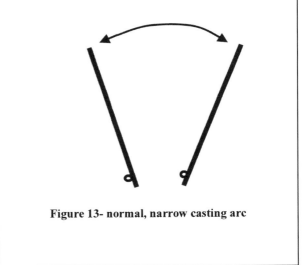

Figure 13- normal, narrow casting arc

False casting still requires a whole arm movement. Be sure your forearm and upper arm are moving during false casting. The elbow lifts and lowers as the forearm moves back and forth. Your wrist will move from bent to straight on the stops. Be sure to watch your wrist as you false cast.

Photo series 11- sequence 1-5 ;elbow lifts and lowers, forearm moves back and forth

Many people false cast far too many times. They lose focus and false cast more than necessary. To avoid this, practice false casting a series of 3 or 4 false casts only. This is sufficient to work on your timing, casting arc and loop size, but avoids excessive false casting. When fishing, false cast the minimum number that is required for your goal. When practicing casting, experiment with timing and casting arc to discover their effect on your cast. Having the right timing and right arc is a thing of beauty and people spend their whole lives pursuing this perfection, so enjoy!

False Casting:
- Line hand maintains tension of line
- Monitor line from first stripping guide to line hand
- Line hand and rod hand move in unison
- Trajectory changes, forward cast is more toward the horizon
- Use whole arm movement: elbow lifts and lowers, forearm moves toward and away from body, wrist opens and closes on the stops
- Watch loop size and shape to adjust casting arc
- Listen to line for timing clues

Shooting Line

After you learn to false cast, you can move to the technique of shooting line. This is when fly casting really gets fun. Shooting line means you can extend the range of your fishing without having to carry that extra line in the air during your cast. It is the energy in the unrolling loop, which pulls the line from your line hand allowing you to shoot line. The first step is to be able to see the loop form after the rod is stopped. When you can recognize this, you are ready to shoot line. Watch your rod tip when false casting and see that the loop is formed after you stop the rod (both forward and backward). Watch the loop form and unroll. When you can see the loop, this means you have stopped your rod well. The rod has been loaded and unloaded.

Photo 19-start position for shooting line

In order to have line available to shoot, pull some additional line off the reel. Start with a small amount of line, approximately four feet. You will have the rod in one hand and the line in the other hand. The line hand will pinch the line tightly. Be sure, there is no slack between the line hand and the stripping guide of the rod. The extra line for shooting will be in a loose loop between your rod hand and line hand.

Photo series 12- L- -line hand pinches fly line; R- line hand maintains tension of fly line

Start by making 2-3 false casts. Watch for the loop to be formed after the stop on the forward cast. When you are can see the loop form after the stop, you can release the line on your next forward cast. False cast as usual. Now when you see the loop has formed, you release line from your line hand and watch for the loop to pull the extra line out. To control the release of the line from your line hand put the tips of your thumb and index finger together to form a circle.

Photo 20- line hand forms a circle

Your line hand can now control the line being shot. Your line hand fingers move from a pinch when holding the line securely to a circle to release the line for shooting. If you simply let go of the line it can jump up and tangle around your reel, rod and hands. It is best to learn to have a controlled shoot.

When practicing shooting line, you may need to work on your timing of the shoot. If you release line too soon, the loop will not have formed and you will not be able to shoot line. If you wait too long, your loop of line will unroll completely and there is no energy left to shoot extra line. Both of these are easy to recognize. The most common mistake when shooting line is not stopping the rod well and try to push the line out the guides. This never works. The rod must be stopped well, meaning a smooth acceleration to an abrupt or complete stop. This is what gives you the good loop with enough energy to shoot line. Practice shooting line on your third false cast. Work on the timing of the release so you shoot all four feet of extra line.

Once you have shot line successfully on your forward delivery cast, you can learn to control the shoot and shoot a small amount of line on each forward cast. This allows you to get the total amount of line you need into your cast as quickly as possible. To shoot line on multiple false casts, your line hand thumb and index finger will alternately pinch tightly or form a circle to alternately hold or release line. On each forward cast, you release a little line. On each back cast, you pinch the line tightly. With this technique, you can shoot just enough line to reach your target. This is truly a controlled shoot.

After you have shot line, and presented the cast, your line hand must return control of the line to the rod hand. The line hand will reach over and place the line under your middle finger of the rod hand. This keeps the line under tension so you can set the hook if a fish eats your fly, or begin to strip the line (more about this in the section on playing fish).

The amount of line you can shoot will be determined in part by the design of your line. Weight forward lines and shooting head lines are designed to shoot the maximum amount of line with the entire weighted section at the rod tip. Double taper lines do not shoot line as well because the weight is not concentrated. The amount of line outside the rod tip will affect the amount of line you can shoot. Remember that the fly line has weight. If you cast more line, you have a greater the load on the rod. This creates more energy for shooting line. The maximum amount of line to false cast will be the head section of the fly line. Keep this weighted section of the fly line close to the rod tip. If the weighted section is very far from the rod tip, then the transfer of energy to the line is not efficient and less line can be released on the shoot. When learning to shoot line, use about 30 feet of fly line for the cast, and shoot a few additional feet. As you improve, you can shoot more with a beginning goal of shooting an additional 10 feet of line.

Shooting Line:
- Watch for loop to form after the stop
- Thumb and index finger pinch fly line during the cast
- Thumb and index finger form a circle to release line for shooting
- Shoot line on multiple forward casts by alternately pinching and releasing line through thumb and index finger of the line hand

Putting it all together: how to fish

The presentation cast delivers your fly to the fish and then you must fish the fly. How you fish the fly will depend on the fishing situation. In some situations, the water will help impart action to your fly. In other scenarios, you must give action to the fly to make it seem alive and appealing to the fish. I will explain the basics of fishing in each of these situations. Keep in mind that this is just to get you started. As you progress as an angler, you will constantly be learning, fine-tuning and customizing your approach to match your fishing needs.

The typical fishing scenario is to start by pulling line off your reel and work that line outside the rod tip by moving the rod back and forth using the resistance of the water to help pull out your line. Use the roll cast to straighten your line. Next, strip off a little more line, and make a few false casts. Shoot line to deliver your fly to your target. Your rod tip should be low to the water. Your line hand has returned the line to your rod hand and your line is trapped under your rod hand middle finger. The line is straight on the water in front of you. This is called tight line fishing. There is no slack in the line and if the fish takes your fly, you should feel this immediately.

At this point, you will need to impart some action to your fly in a technique called stripping. Stripping is the act that imparts action to your fly. You move the fly and line through the water by pulling small amounts of fly line with your line hand. Between strips, the line remains secured under your right hand middle finger. Reach up with the line hand, while the right hand releases tension. The left hand pulls some fly line, from behind the middle finger, to make the fly move. When you have ended the strip, your right hand now provides tension and secures the line while you reach up with your left hand to pull more line and move your fly again. The length of the strip will vary as you match the natural conditions. You match the speed of movement of the fly to the actual food items in the area and the speed of any current.

This process is repeated until either a fish takes your fly, or you have stripped in the line so only a foot remains outside the rod tip. If the fish takes your fly then you must set the hook. If your fly was not taken, you must start the entire process over again. Wiggle line out through the guides and roll cast to straighten your line. Make a false cast and shoot some line when you present the fly. Now begin stripping the fly to give it action.

If a fish takes your fly you must set the hook. How you do this depends on the type of fish. When fishing for trout or smaller freshwater bass and lake fish, you can set the hook by quickly lifting up the rod tip when you feel the fish has eaten the fly. This takes out any slack and drives the point of the hook into the fish's mouth. If you are fishing in saltwater or for larger freshwater bass, you need to use a technique called the strip-strike. When stripping the fly and you feel the fish take the fly, continue the strip with your line hand by stripping a little longer. Strip until you feel the hook grab in the fishes mouth. The hook set generally inspires your fish to run for his life so be ready for the fish to take off.

When the fish runs, you must let him do this. If you hold tightly, the fish will break off, and you have nothing. When the fish runs, allow him to run away and have your reel hand off the reel so you do not get your knuckles cut by the reel knob. When the fish settles down and stops running, you can again hold the reel knob and start to reel the fish in. Remember to keep tension on the fish by keeping a bend in the rod. With the rod bent, keep the rod at a 45° angle to the fish. This is a good general rule. This uses your rod to help you apply pressure to the fish. You want to tire the fish so you can land him quickly, revive and release him.

As you play the fish, he may run away several times during the fight. You must let him run each time. Typically, the subsequent runs get progressively shorter as your fish tires. Remember not to fight the fish to exhaustion. The point of catch and release is to allow the fish to live, not to release him ready to die.

Sometimes the fish is too small to run away from you. In this case, continue stripping the fish in. Keep the rod tip up and a 45 ° angle of the rod butt to the fish. When you have about four feet of line remaining outside the rod tip, reach your rod over and behind your line hand side shoulder. This brings the fish in close to you, and you can grab the leader.

With the leader in your hand, can reach down and lift the fish. Trout are best handled by first wetting your hands then cradling the fish to lift him sideways. You can lift stripers and freshwater bass by their jaw. Always be sure your fish does not have teeth before you stick your thumb inside their mouths. Now remove the hook by backing the hook out on the same path it took to be placed. You can use forceps in freshwater or pliers in saltwater. Next, revive the fish by pushing him forward so water will travel through his gills. The fish is ready to be released when he wiggles and tries to get out of your hands. Watch your fish swim away, and you will feel good about contributing to nature. Now it is time to check your leader and fly. If they show damage, change them. Then get back fishing again!

Freshwater Lakes

The above scenario works well for fishing lakes. This is called tight line fishing. You do not want slack in the line at any time. If there is slack, the fish is likely to spit the hook and free himself. I encourage everyone to spend some time fishing on a lake to get experience with a real fishing situation. You can learn a lot on the first few fish you hook, play and land. I suggest using Poppers, a type of top water fly that works well for sunfish and bass. With these flies, you can watch the effect of your stripping action on the fly. In addition, you will generally see the fish eat your fly and the take can be ferocious. This is a great way to get real fishing experience.

Surf/Ocean

Some people will choose to start their fly fishing with striped bass and ocean fishing. The fly casting concepts are the same. The difference is the flies are larger and the gear is usually heavier. It can be a slightly more challenging way to start. When fishing in the ocean, you always have to contend with the surf. This means that the ocean generally works against you and your desire for tight line, no slack fishing. The ocean is always moving so you must constantly watch your line to eliminate slack. This requires frequent use of the roll cast to straighten your line and stripping to remove slack is needed. When you hook a striper, remember to use the strip-strike. In addition, when it is time to land your fish, if you are wading, you may want to move back toward the shore so you can more easily play and land your fish.

Streams & Rivers

When fishing in a stream for trout, small mouth bass, or steelhead. Presentation is critical. When you start fishing the current of the stream can help you. As you pull line out the current will help pull the line straight, downstream. This helps you start casting without slack line. When fishing in a stream, you do not want a tight line to your fly. Generally, stream fishing involves making your fly look like a natural insect or stage of insect, which is travelling in the current unimpeded, without drag. When you drift your fly in the current, it is called a drag free drift. Because your fly should not have drag, the longer the drag free drift, the more water you cover with a natural looking fly. Drag free drift does not happen by chance. As soon as your fly hits the water, it is at risk for drag. Your job in a stream is to take measures to reduce drag and have your fly appear more natural.

One of the most common ways to reduce drag is by making a mend. A mend is an adjustment of the fly line to help your fly float downstream in a natural looking way. The mend is accomplished by using your rod to lift some fly line off the water. Then use a flick of your wrist to reposition the line. If you want the fly to move more quickly, you make a downstream mend. If you want the fly to move more slowly, you make an upstream mend. If the stream has many different currents with different speeds, you may make a series of mends, some upstream some downstream. You do whatever it takes to get that drag free drift for the fly. If you are fishing upstream, (you are facing upstream), it can be easier to get a drag free drift, but you must manage your slack. If you are fishing downstream (you are facing downstream) make sure your fly travels down the stream ahead of your leader and fly line. This is your drag free drift to help you catch more fish.

Changing Direction

When fly fishing you will need to change the direction of your fly and line. In a river, this occurs at the end of every drift when you move from an upstream to a downstream position and want to reposition your fly. You may also want to change the position of your fly if you see a fish in a different place than where you initially put your fly. In both of these situations, you will need a change of direction to reposition your fly to the new location. The simplest way to change direction is by false casting. When false casting, you can make small angles of change with each false cast to reposition your fly. If you are changing from your right to your left, make a back cast to pick up the line. While the back cast is unrolling, make a small angle of change toward your new target area. Then make the forward cast. Repeat this scenario until you have changed position to be in line with your new target area. Remember to change direction while the back cast unrolls. Be sure to look forward at your next forward cast position before making the forward cast. Although it takes a few false casts to accomplish this change, this is a skill you already possess and another great use for false casting.

Advanced Concepts

Accuracy

Photo 21-thumb aims cast, back and forward

Accuracy is controlling the placement of your fly. In order to be successful in fly casting you must be able to place your fly where you want it, where you think the fish is located. Your fly casting should always involve casting to a target. This is the way you will improve your accuracy. To be accurate in fly casting you need to remember a few concepts. First, always select a specific target and use your thumb to aim the cast. The smaller the target area the more difficult it is to be accurate, so start with a three foot circle. As you improve, you can work with smaller targets to improve your accuracy skills. Next, consider that it will be easier to be accurate if you move your rod in a straight line toward the target. The thumb on top of the rod butt gives you a way to easily move your rod in a straight line either toward or away from your target. Use your thumb as an aiming device to help "sight" the cast. This creates a hand-target straight line.

Stand looking directly at the target and determine the straight line from your eye to the target. This line of sight from your eye to the target creates another straight line, called your eye-target line. To be highly accurate, be sure that the straight line from your rod hand to the target and the straight line from your eye to the target will intersect right at the target.

Photo 22-hand-target line & eye target line meet at target

Keeping your rod hand and thumb close to the eye you use for sighting the target, will keep these two straight lines closer together. This facilitates your accuracy. The key to accuracy is determining the two straight lines: your hand-target line and your eye-target line, then being sure these two straight lines meet or intersect right at the target.

Trajectory

Trajectory refers to the angle of the cast. The most efficient fly casting occurs along a straight line. This straight line is on some angle both away from and toward your target. A longer line with a more distant the target, requires a shallow casting trajectory. For targets that are closer, and you are casting shorter lengths of line, the angle or trajectory of the cast is steeper. One of your goals in fly casting is to determine the correct trajectory for the cast. With a little of practice at both near and distant targets you will have a better sense of the range of angles for your cast.

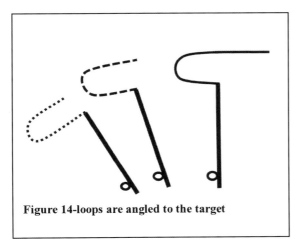

Figure 14-loops are angled to the target

Photo series 13- trajectory top to bottom: close, moderate, distant

Off shoulder & Casting in All Planes

Photo 23-- vertical position

If there is wind or obstacles on your rod hand side, it will be useful to learn the off shoulder casting position. Off shoulder casting is using your dominant arm to cast the line from the non-dominant side of your body. For right-handed casters this means a cast with your right hand, but with the line and rod positioned on the left side of your body. Change your stance to facilitate straight line casting. Place your left foot back a little further back than your right. Rotate your shoulders and hips so the right side is more forward. Your rod hand and forearm tilt in toward your body while your elbow tips away. Now cast as usual and the fly line will be on your off shoulder, free of wind or obstacles. This is the basis for being able to cast in all planes or angles. The casting plane is the angle of your cast. The easiest way to understand casting angles is to think about casting in front of a clock face. Straight ahead is the 12 o'clock position. Ideally, you want to be able to cast at any position from 3 o'clock to 9 o'clock. To cast toward your right, (1, 2 or 3 o'clock) you tilt your forearm and hand away

Photo series 14- L- off vertical; R- nearly horizontal

from your body. Your elbow moves in toward your body. To cast on the off shoulder, left side (11, 10 or 9 o'clock) rotate your hand and forearm in, while your elbow tilts out. When casting off your left shoulder, be sure to keep your right hand in front of your face to facilitate moving in a straight line.

Summary:

To be successful in fly casting you must master the casts and techniques presented in lesson one. These represent the minimum skill set you need to be independent. Your local fly shop will help supplement your fishing knowledge and provide advice. Hiring a guide will shorten the learning curve and improve your fishing success immediately. However, you alone are responsible for the casting and will need to meet this challenge. You will never be successful as a fly caster or fly fisherman if you do not practice the skills which have been presented. Because it is fishing, people expect the skills to come naturally, but they do not. In golf it is customary to take many lessons and spend hours practicing shots. If you could spend just some of that time practicing your fly casting skills, you will be rewarded tenfold both in enjoyment, fish, and a lifetime of outdoor experiences. Use the suggestions for lesson one in the practice section of this book.

Minimum skill set for beginner:
- Two casts:
    1) Roll Cast
    2) Basic Cast
- Two techniques:
    1) False Cast
    2) Shoot Line

Lesson 2: Intermediate Fly Casting: Beyond the Basics

After your first lesson and a little bit of practice you are ready to fish. You can fish very successfully before you feel the need to improve your fly casting skills. At some time, most people reach a point where they feel they could or should be better with their casting. This generally occurs when they challenge their current casting skills. This challenge can come from fishing under more adverse weather conditions; more difficult fishing environments such as larger bodies of water; casting larger flies that are more air resistant; targeting more difficult species of fish; or needing to cast further distance. All of these situations present a challenge to your current skill level and require you to develop your casting abilities.

As you progress from beginner to intermediate, your need for casting instruction changes. As a beginner, you are a clean slate. You have little if any prior knowledge of casting. You need a very specific set of guidelines that tells you how to move your body to make the cast. As an intermediate caster, you focus less on how to move your body, and more on the concepts of executing a good cast. You need a higher level of understanding about how the cast is made. You will need to identify both the fundamental needs for all casts and the variables, which are adjusted and balanced to achieve a good cast. Once you understand these fundamental principles and variables, then focus on ensuring they occur, you will increase your casting efficiency and see immediate results.

As an intermediate caster, you will also want to add more complex casting techniques, and learn the hauls and advanced shooting line. Before adding hauls, you will benefit from refining your basic casting principles. Improving your efficiency with the basics will allow you to get the most benefit from the additional techniques.

This lesson starts with a discussion of the five essential components of every straight line cast. This provides some physics as a base for what makes your casting work. It also gives you a framework to analyze your cast. You can determine what you are doing well or what to improve. Take your time with this material and proceed, as you are ready. Because this is a progressive learning approach, you may find it helpful to review material from the first lesson before starting this lesson.

Style versus Substance

As an experienced caster, you have developed a way of moving your body to make the cast; this is the style part of fly casting. As long as your style is working, and you get the needed results, you can maintain this. If your style is impeding your casting abilities, then it is time for a change. There are times when a particular style may help you achieve a substantive issue. In this case, I have included style options to help you achieve better results.

Substance refers to the fundamental principles that all good fly casts have in common. The fundamental principles are known to as the essentials of a fly cast; these are the core ingredients of all casts. The more efficiently you accomplish each of the essentials, the more efficient your cast, and the more you can accomplish with your casting. There are five essentials for any fly cast. These essentials are agreed upon by most fly casting gurus (acknowledged by the Federation of Fly Fishers) and are worthy of an in depth look.

Five Essentials for All Fly Casts

1) Straight line path of the rod tip

The rod tip must move in a straight line path throughout the cast. A straight line is the shortest path between the start and stop position of your rod. The fly line follows the rod tip path, so a straight line path represents the most efficient path for your cast. Moving the rod tip in a straight line helps keeps the fly line under tension, which is the basis for loading the rod. The most common way to go off this straight path is by twisting the body during the back cast or forward cast.

First, you need to determine if this is a problem for you. To judge if you are casting on a straight line, use a straight line on your rod hand side. You can use a painted line on the ground such as on an athletic field or place a length of rope on the ground beside you.

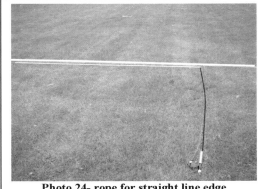
Photo 24- rope for straight line edge

Use the straight line as an edge to judge your rod tip path. Start by making a back cast and stop. Allow the line to fall down behind you. Turn and look at your fly line to see the placement of the line. It should be in parallel with the edge of your straight line. If your fly line is parallel, then your rod moved in a straight line. If the fly line is at an angle or crosses the straight-line edge, then you are not moving in a straight line and likely have a twist. This twisting is more common when you cast in an open stance, with an off vertical angle to your side. To resolve this twisting, cast in a vertical stance. The vertical stance keeps your shoulders, hips and feet square to the target. This keeps your forearm and hand in line with your upper arm. As you move your rod arm to make the cast, keep your rod arm in line with your rod shoulder and upper arm. When you cast in this stance, you use your body structure to facilitate moving in a straight line.

Photo 25-vertical position using body to guide straight path

If you prefer to cast using the open stance, use your straight line edge as a guide for your rod tip to follow. While making the back cast you use the rope as a guide for your rod tip. Watch the rope while you cast, move your hand in a direction that keeps the rod tip in line with the rope. This will be easiest to see if you cast in a horizontal plane, but can be done at any angle. Use this straight line edge when practicing to train your muscles to move in a straight line.

Now evaluate your forward cast. Use the straight line edge to evaluate. Make a back cast and allow it to fall. Walk forward to remove slack line and make your forward cast. Use the rope as a guide for the straight line and the end of the rope is your target. Make your forward cast allowing it to fall and see how the fly line lays out. The fly line should fall in a parallel line with your rope. If it does not, then you have a twist on the forward cast. To resolve this, again use your rope as a straight line edge and cast in the vertical position to use your body alignment or using the open stance, with a casting angle that allows you to see the rod tip move along the straight line edge.

When casting in the vertical plane, stand so the rope is just beside your rod hand. This will keep the rope in line with your shoulder and hips on your rod hand side. In the off vertical plane, watch the straight line as you make the cast being sure you move the rod tip along this straight line.

Casting in the open stance with an off vertical angle, you may notice your line landing to the left of the line. This is a slice. In this case, you may have started on a straight line, but completed your cast by twisting your rod hand toward the line hand side of your body. This causes your fly and line to be directed to the left. To resolve this use the end of your rope as a target, and aim the cast at the rope, this should eliminate the slice.

Another common way to come off the straight line path is to stop the rod tip too low on either the back cast on the forward or delivery cast. This results in a large, open loop. On the back cast, your fly may hit the ground or water behind you. This is a result of stopping your rod with the rod tip aimed downward. To resolve this you need to think about aiming your back cast. Use your thumb as your focus for aiming. Imagine there is a straight line, which extends from the thumb pad in front and the thumbnail behind you. When you stop the back cast, the imaginary line from your thumbnail should be opposite your forward cast target area, not pointed down. I suggest you review the information about aiming, in the casting concepts section of the book.

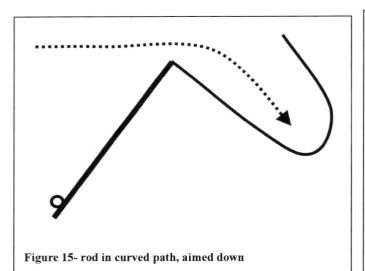

Figure 15- rod in curved path, aimed down

Photo 26-- imaginary line off thumb for aiming

On the forward cast, if you see a wide open loop, look at your thumb to evaluate the trajectory of the imaginary line from your thumb pad. If you stop with the thumb aimed downward, that is where you cast will go. If your thumb is aimed downward, you may have moved the rod tip in a curved path rather than the straight path.

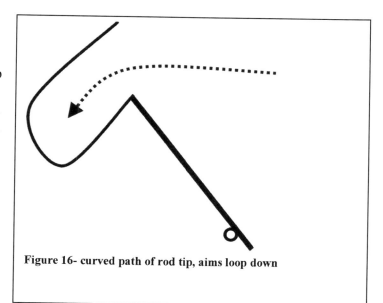

Figure 16- curved path of rod tip, aims loop down

To resolve this situation be sure your trajectory to the target is a straight line directly to the target. You do not cast along a straight line, and then aim downward to the target. Rather the straight line of your cast includes your target. The straight line is directly toward and ends at your target. Place a target at the end of your straight line to see the continuum of the straight line to your target. Now cast along the straight line directly to your target. Remember to watch for your loop to be aimed at your target. Your loop should unroll in line with your target. Using targets and casting in the horizontal plane is the easiest way to focus on straight line casting. To focus on this in the vertical plane, practice casting to targets at different heights. This will help you adjust the straight line needed for your target. (See practice section exercise)

2) Slack line is kept to a minimum

The fly cast is a system that works by being under tension. The rod cannot begin to load until the line leader and fly are all under tension. Slack line represents a lack of tension and the rod cannot load, so slack is to be avoided. Slack can be introduced in many places in the cast. The most common places for slack to appear are at the start of the back cast and with poor timing between the back cast and forward cast. When making a back cast, start with the line straight in front of you. Before you make the cast, look at your rod tip. The rod tip should be very close to the water when you start your back cast. Frequently, anglers get in the habit of starting with their rod tip several feet above the water. This creates

Photo 27-rod tip low to water to avoid slack line

slack, limits your casting stroke and is inefficient. To solve this train your eyes to look at the placement of your rod tip before you start your back cast and be sure it is just above or in the water. Be sure to have your fly line straight before beginning your back cast. Start your cast with the rod tip low. The rod can start to load immediately, and the cast is more efficient.

        Slack related to poor timing can occur if you pause too long between the back and

forward casts. You need to pause to allow the fly line loop to unroll. If you pause too long, the line looses tension and slack is created. There is only a moment when the loop has unrolled and the fly line is straight in the air behind you. After this moment, gravity takes over and the line starts to fall. If you pause too long, the line falls, and you have slack. Your timing may be too slow if your fly hits the water in front of you as you false cast, or if your flies have dull hooks from hitting rocks behind you. To correct your timing, watch the fly line loop as it unrolls. Watching the loop on the forward cast is easy. To watch the loop on the back cast, use the open stance. After the back cast, rotate your neck and head so your eyes can watch the loop unroll. You are watching to anticipate the loop being fully unrolled. If you wait until you see the loop completely unroll, it will be too late. It takes too

Photo 28- slack line from poor timing

much time for your eyes to see and register with your brain that the loop has unrolled, and it is time to start forward. Rather, you need to anticipate the loop's full unrolling. As the loop unrolls watch for the loop to change for a long oval to a sideways capital letter J or candy cane shape. You are looking for the last 1-2 feet of fly line before the line-leader connection. When the loop has unrolled to this point, it is time to start your forward cast. Using this visual cue will help you develop good timing.

        To practice this use the open stance and watch for this candy cane shape as your indication to start the next cast. By the time, you see the loop has almost unrolled turn your

head forward to aim the forward cast. The loop will have completely unrolled and you will have good timing.

        You can also improve your timing by relaxing your rod hand grip after the stop. Develop the ability to feel the rod vibrations cease when the line has unrolled. With a relaxed hand, you can feel when the shocking stop of the rod has dissipated and the loop has unrolled. When you learn to feel this in your rod butt, you will develop your timing to precision.

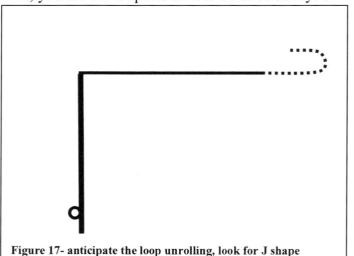

Figure 17- anticipate the loop unrolling, look for J shape

Poor timing from too short a pause is easy to recognize by a cracking sound. If your pause is too short, the fly line is moving in two directions, at once. With the line moving both backward and forward, it causes the line to snap around from one direction to the next. This is usually self-limiting because you snap off your fly and most people will learn to slow down.

Timing is a variable that must be matched to a given cast. A shorter length of line takes less time to unroll, so a shorter pause is needed. Longer lengths of line take more time to unroll and need a longer pause. The wind conditions may affect the timing by increasing or decreasing the rate of the loop unrolling. Remember that timing is a variable that adjusts to the particular cast.

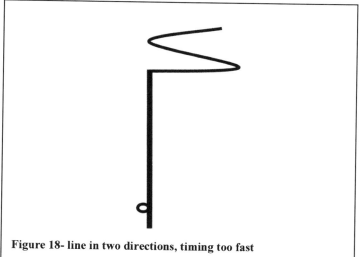

Figure 18- line in two directions, timing too fast

3) Casting stroke starts slowly and is an overall acceleration to an abrupt stop

The nature of the casting stroke is an overall acceleration to an abrupt stop. The acceleration of the rod as it pulls against the weight and inertia of the fly line creates the loading or bending of the rod. The abrupt stop unloads the rod transferring the energy from the bent rod to the fly line. This creates the loop and propels the loop in a direction. Both the overall acceleration and the abrupt stop are critical to efficient fly casting. The most common ways this principle is violated are by starting the casting stroke too quickly, casting too fast, or not stopping abruptly.

The casting stroke must be an acceleration. It is not simply moving the rod fast. The casting stroke needs to start slowly getting the line, leader and fly moving in a direction. This is the loading move, getting all the parts under tension so the rod can bend. The casting stroke continues with a gradual increase in speed until the stop. Most casters use too much speed and start the stroke too quickly, relying of speed to make the rod bend. Starting the casting stroke too quickly is problematic because the faster you are moving your rod arm; the more difficult it is to control the path of the rod. It is more difficult to stop along the straight line when moving fast. It requires more precision. It is also more difficult to be smooth when you are moving fast. This is common for casters who use their strength to move the rod, rather than finesse to build acceleration.

You can recognize speed in your cast by the sound the rod makes as you move it through the air. If the rod makes a harsh whooshing sound, like a strong winter wind, then you are forcing yourself on the cast. You are using your strength to move the rod forcefully through the stroke. To solve this too fast movement you need to slow down your cast. Focus on getting the rod to bend, then pulling deeper into the bend.

Make a cast as usual and listen for the sound of the cast. Now make the same cast with the same amount of line, but try to use half of that speed. Repeat the cast using half as much speed again. Now make the cast using as little speed as possible. Use only enough speed to move the line which causes the rod to bend (you're still accelerating, just ending at a lower overall speed), notice how slowly you can move to make the cast. By slowing down, you can concentrate on acceleration as a way to make the rod bend rather than just being fast. When you start the casting stroke more slowly, you can build the acceleration gradually in a controlled manner. This is better suited to controlling the long flexible weight of your fly line.

Most intermediate casters have only one speed of casting stroke. This can be too much for one cast and insufficient for another. The casting stroke acceleration must be varied. Just as a car that can accelerate at a variety of speeds: (5 mph, 10 mph or 15 mph) you will want to develop a range of speeds for your casting stroke acceleration. Your goal is to select the appropriate rate of acceleration for each cast. Only by exploring the minimum acceleration and speed required for a cast will you be able to develop a range of acceleration. The common theme is to start slowly and build the speed gradually until the stop. It is not speed which loads the rod, but the increase in speed, the acceleration.

The stop ends the casting stroke and forms your loop. If you stop the rod by gradually slowing down, the rod unloads gradually. You lose some of the energy in the rod and have less energy in your cast. An abrupt stop of the rod maximizes the transfer of energy from the rod to the fly line. If your loop barely unrolls, or seems to collapse, you are likely slowing down gradually, not stopping abruptly.

The acceleration during the casting stroke must continue right up to the stop. The stop is a definitive moment in time. At the stop, all movements should cease. You should feel like a mime: you are moving one moment and the next you are like a freeze frame, frozen in time. This cessation of movement is critical to your fly cast. When your stop is this abrupt and preceded by continuous acceleration, your line will form a tight loop with enough energy to unroll completely.

As you are focusing on smooth acceleration, not speed, you can cast with less tension in both your rod hand and arm. This allows you to have more control during the stop phase of your casting stroke. To help you stop the rod abruptly you can use hand tension. During the casting stroke, your hand should be relaxed. At the stop, your hand can squeeze tightly to ensure a complete stop. On the back cast stop, your hand squeezes to a stop and your arm muscles tighten to help stop all motions. After the stop, relax your hand and arm to feel the loop unroll and develop your timing. On the forward cast stop, you use all the muscles of your hand and wrist. Your thumb pushes forward while your lower fingers pull back; this causes a quick rotation of the rod butt to a position that is parallel with your forearm. The structure of your forearm and hand forces the rod butt to stop. During this wrist rotation, the rod tip quickly accelerates to a stop, unloading the energy to your fly line.

4) Power must be applied smoothly and gradually

In order for the fly cast to be perfect, the power must be applied gradually. If you apply power in any type of erratic nature, the loop will suffer. You can see this by watching your fly cast loop. Power that is applied smoothly and gradually yields a nice smooth unrolling loop, the loop we all dream of. A loop that kicks or has waves and bumps as it unrolls results from uneven or excessive power. The most common ways that power is not applied smoothly include starting the casting stroke to quickly, starting fast then slowing down, or punching the cast on the delivery.

The casting stroke does need to accelerate and have some speed, but if you start too fast, your rod tip may flex erratically. It is similar accelerating your car from a stoplight so quickly that you leave a rubber mark from your tires. Just like with your car, you need to start slowly and accelerate gradually over some distance. Your goal is to be smooth. Mentally, you should think about a smooth sweep of your rod arm in line with your target to the stop.

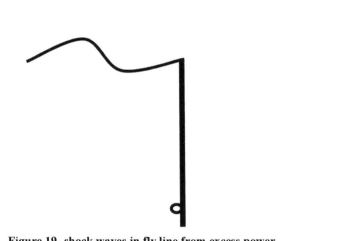

Figure 19- shock waves in fly line from excess power

If you start the stroke too quickly, you are likely to get a tailing loop. A tailing loop is a closed loop. It occurs because the rod tip has moved in a curved path. The over acceleration at the start of the casting stroke causes erratic flexing of the rod tip. This results in a curved, concave path and a tailing loop.

Starting the casting stroke at one speed, then slowing down rather than continuing acceleration will also cause the rod to flex erratically. The rod tip will move in a curved path and yield a tailing loop. You need to focus on being smooth with your casting stroke. Focus on smoothness of acceleration not speed and your loops should improve.

When casting longer distances it is common to get a tailing loop by punching or hitting the cast with excess power at the end. In this situation, the caster knows they need a deeper load in the rod to get more energy into their fly line. Wanting more rod bend, they give the cast a burst of power at the end of the cast. This burst of power results in an erratic flex of the rod tip. This yields a curved path of the rod tip and a tailing loop. The solution is not adding extra power. The final delivery cast should have no more power than the last false cast. Focus on the delivery cast as feeling similar to the false casts. Trick your mind into this by false casting and simply delivering the final cast. Do not wind up or anticipate it. Again, focus on being smooth. Excess energy will only detract from that perfect cast. To get the deeper load in the rod for more distance you will need to consider the last essential, which is stroke length.

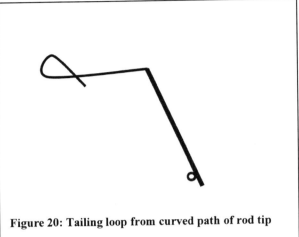

Figure 20: Tailing loop from curved path of rod tip

5) The casting stroke length and casting arc must vary in proportion to the length of line being cast

Stroke length and casting arc are both variables, which must be adjusted for the amount of line you are casting. A short cast needs a short stroke and a narrow arc. A longer cast needs a longer stroke with a wider arc. The casting arc is the angle of the rod butt at the start and stop positions of each cast. The arc must be of sufficient width to accommodate the amount of bend in the rod, yet narrow enough to ensure the straight line path of the rod tip. The casting arc must adjust because the rod, bends under the weight of the fly line. The rod will bend less with a shorter line, and more with a longer line. The shorter line has less weight to bend the rod, and the longer line has more weight and more rod bend.

The casting stroke length will be shorter for a short length of line and longer for longer length of line. If you have a short length of line, you can build the needed acceleration and rod loading in a shorter distance and still be smooth. For a longer cast you still need to build the acceleration smoothly. You want a greater bend in the rod so more stroke length is needed to get this deeper bend in a smooth manner.

Photo series 15- L- short line, short stroke: R- longer line, longer stroke, wider arc

The most common way this principle is violated is by using too short of a stroke for the amount of line being cast. Many casters become comfortable with one stroke length and one casting arc. When they cast greater distances, these presets no longer work for them. This is frequently seen when you begin casting 40-50 ft of line and you are getting a tailing loop because the stroke length is too short.

To address the need for a longer casting stroke, you can add body movement to your casting. To lift a longer length of line on your back cast, bend your knees and lean forward before starting your pick up. This leaning forward can add a foot to your stroke length. After the back cast, you can add a relaxing or leaning backwards while the cast is unrolling. You must stop first, and then lean backwards while the cast unrolls. This will give you additional stroke length for the forward cast. Next, you can false cast with the leaning motion both forward and backward. This helps smoothly develop the increased load you need and helps those longer strokes feel more fluid.

To develop the range of casting stroke lengths and casting arcs, also work with shorter lengths of line. Use about 20 feet of line and false cast. Use just enough casting

Photo series 16- body movement to add stroke length

arc and stroke length to make smooth loops. Focus on how short of a stroke length and narrow of a casting arc is needed for this short line. Now return to the longer line and you will be more aware of the range of stroke length and casting arc you can use.

The angle of the casting arc must match your length of line as well. For short casts the trajectory of the cast should be steeper and the casting arc must be tipped forward to represent the straight line trajectory which matches the closer target. The casting arc will look more like a capital letter V. In distance casting, the target is further away and the trajectory is flatter. The casting arc may seem perpendicular to the ground. For longer distances, the casting arc should look less like a capital letter V and more like a wide V that has a flat base. Develop this wider casting arc and longer casting stroke and you will have a smoother distance casts.

Understanding the essential elements of a cast will improve your efficiency and prepare you to handle the difficulties of wind and adding the techniques of hauling and shooting line.

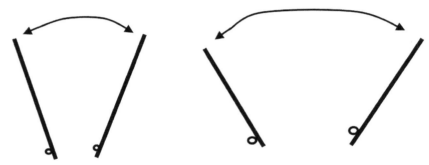

Figure 21 -narrow arc needed for short lengths of line   Figure 22- wider arc needed for longer lengths of line

Five Essentials of a good cast:
1) Straight line path of the rod tip
2) Slack line is kept to a minimum
3) Casting stroke starts slowly and is an overall acceleration to an abrupt stop
4) Power must be applied smoothly and gradually
5) Casting stroke length and casting arc must vary in proportion to the line being cast

Wind

Most fly fisherman find the wind to be a challenge and seek to improve their abilities to cast in windy conditions. The wind can come from all points of the compass, and you need to be able to handle wind from any direction. To be successful in dealing with the wind, you need to determine the effect the wind will have on your cast and make adjustments to counteract this effect. In all windy situations, you will want high line speed to better control the fly line; tight loops to be aerodynamic and cut through the wind; and consider a change in trajectory, timing or casting plane. These are the key adjustments for handling any wind condition. The major direction for wind is from the four quadrants: head winds, tailwinds, wind from rod arm or line hand side. Apply the necessary changes and you will improve your ability to fly cast in the wind.

Head winds

With the wind blowing in your face, your fly line will tend to be blown back at you. To handle this situation you want a tight loop with more speed. To get a tighter loop: adjust your casting arc so it is only as wide as needed, and cast along a straight line, directly to the target. You also need to adjust the trajectory. You will want to aim the cast on a steeper downward angle

Photo series 17- L- low angle for head wind; R- crouch to keep cast low

and have your loop unroll inches above the water. Use a higher rate of acceleration and cast a little faster to get the higher line speed. This combination of adjustments helps your loop cut into the wind better and helps you cast in head winds.

Photo 29-side arm into wind

You can also cast in the horizontal plane and make a sidearm cast. This presents a low profile to the wind. You can take advantage of lower wind strength just above the water's surface. This also allows you to tuck your cast under objects.

Tailwinds

When the wind comes from behind you, the back cast will not want to unroll. This wind causes problems with keeping the line under tension. To accommodate this wind, you will adjust your timing so the pause on the back cast is not as long. You will again change the trajectory of the cast. On the back cast, you can aim the cast more overhead, stopping the rod, not beyond a 12 o'clock position (imaginary clock face is beside you). On the forward cast, you can aim your cast well above your target. This allows the wind to help your cast unroll before it falls to the water on the delivery. Tailwinds require a steep trajectory back cast, a shorter pause and a forward cast aimed to allow the wind to help unroll the loop.

Photo series 18- L- steep trajectory back cast; R- aim forward cast high

Another option for dealing with tailwinds is to make two forward casts. Turn to stand sideways to your target. Make a forward cast to your right side. While the cast is unrolling, rotate your hand and forearm to make a forward cast in the other direction, toward your left hand side. After the hand and forearm rotate, bring the elbow back in by your side and complete your forward cast to the left side. This is a very effective technique for tailwinds as it uses the strength of your muscles in the forward direction to cast into the tailwind.

Photo series 19- top: L-R: - cast away from target, rotate arm & turn head as cast unrolls to set up for forward delivery cast; bottom: L-R forward delivery cast to target

Wind on the rod hand side

If the wind is from your right (rod arm side), the line and fly may get blown into you. For these winds, you will want to place the line on your left hand or downwind side. Use the off shoulder stance. Put your left foot slightly back and turn your shoulders and hips to the left. Tilt your rod arm in front of your face, allowing your elbow to leave your side. This will keep you aligned with your target and the fly line away from your body.

Photo 30-off shoulder keeps line away from wind

Another useful technique in fishing with these winds is to use your back cast to deliver the fly. If you have very strong winds from your rod hand side, use this back cast delivery. Stand sideways to your target, so the cast will be on the downwind side. Cast as usual, but when you stop the rod on the back cast hold that position. Allow the loop to unroll and follow the rod tip down to present and fish your fly.

Photo 31- use back cast to deliver the fly

Wind on your line hand side

The biggest concern with winds from the line hand side is the ability to place your fly accurately. The wind will blow your fly down wind, off target to the right. To adjust for the wind, false cast above a different target. Judge how far to the right the wind will move your fly. When you present your fly, aim the fly upwind of the target that same distance. When the wind affects your fly, it will be blown down wind, right on your target. Keep in mind when false casting to judge the effect of the wind do not cast above your fishing target. Pick another target area simply to determine the wind's effect. When you have determined the needed upwind adjustment, you can deliver your fly to the fish.

Combination winds

When the winds blow from an angle such as northeast or southwest, you will want to consider a change in casting plane to cast at an angle to the wind. The casting angle may be on your dominant side or off shoulder side depending on the wind. Select an angle to help your cast slice into the wind. Remember to use high line speed and the straight line to the target area for a tight loop.

Wind Direction	Problem	Solution
Headwinds	Fly and line blown back at you	<ul><li>High line speed, tight loop</li><li>Steep trajectory, unrolling just above the target</li><li>Side arm cast</li></ul>
Tailwinds	Wind prevents back cast from unrolling	<ul><li>Do not stop beyond 12 o'clock position on back cast, do not wait for cast to fully unroll, aim forward cast higher to allow wind to help cast unroll</li><li>Use 2 forward casts</li></ul>
Wind on rod hand side	Line and fly blown into caster	<ul><li>Cast in off shoulder stance</li><li>Deliver the fly on the back cast</li></ul>
Winds on line hand side	Fly blown downwind of target	<ul><li>Aim upwind of target to adjust for wind blowing line off target</li></ul>

The Hauls: Single and Double

The double haul is a technique that most fly casters hope to master. Most advanced casters gravitate to using the double haul with all their casts. Done correctly it makes all casts easier. If you attempt the double haul before you have solid fundamentals you are likely to stifle the development of your casting mechanics and use the double haul as a crutch, casting your mistakes farther. Once you have your fundamental casting mechanics in place, the double haul is a fantastic asset to your casting arsenal.

The haul is a tug on the fly line during the casting stroke. The haul is useful because it shares the work of loading the fly rod between both hands; increases line speed and forms tighter loops. With the haul, you can use a shorter casting stroke. This is helpful in tight fishing situations when you are wading deep or positioned in a way that your stroke length is limited. The increased loading of the rod with the haul, is also helpful with distance casting because for the same stroke length, you get a deeper load in the rod, which allows you to have more energy in your loop and shoot more line for longer distance. Increased line speed is beneficial when lifting heavy, air resistant flies off the water, trying to lift a sinking fly line, or when need your loop to cut through the wind. The tighter loop from the double haul keeps the energy in your loop concentrated in the nose of the loop. It more efficiently directs the energy of the cast toward the target. This helps in wind or with shooting line for distance. There are two main types of hauls, a single haul and a double haul. I use the definition of a single haul as a one-direction move, a haul with no give back. The double haul has two moves. It is a haul and a give back of that line.

The haul is a pull on the fly line during the casting stroke, and occurs at a very specific time. The haul is coordinated with the stop. The key concept is that both the line hand and the rod hand move in the same direction in the beginning of the casting stroke to start the loading of the rod. The haul occurs in coordination with the stop. During the loading move, the hands move in unison. They separate on the stop.

Photo series 20- L- hands move in same direction to begin cast; R- hands separate on the stop

Within the casting stroke, the moving of the rod to get it loaded is the longest portion. The stop and haul are relatively short in comparison to the overall stroke length. The haul length is matched to the length of the stop. The rod arm's wrist rotation starts when your thumb is 90° from your target (back cast or forward cast). This is when your haul should start. The haul lasts as long as the wrist rotation. The haul accelerates to a stop. This acceleration to a stop lasts as long as the wrist rotation of the rod arm. Because the rod arm is moving within the casting stroke, and the wrist rotation of the stop occurs within this movement, the wrist rotation occurs over a few inches. It is not a stop in place. The wrist rotation occurs within the stroke. If the stop is short, with a rotation occurring of a short distance, then the haul is also short. If the stop occurs over a longer distance, the haul will be longer. When the rod hand has completed the stop, the line hand completes the haul. Both movements end at the same point in time. The stop and haul are coordinated and matched both to each other and to the length of line, you are casting. A short cast needs a short haul and a longer cast needs a longer haul.

Like the casting stroke, the haul of the line is an acceleration to a stop. Its speed is matched to the acceleration of the rod. A fast casting stroke has a quicker haul. A slower tempo casting stroke can have a slower tempo of the haul.

The haul occurs in a direction opposite the rod hand. On the back cast, the rod hand moves up and back on an inclining trajectory behind you. The haul with the line hand is forward and slightly downward. On the forward cast, the rod hand is moving forward and outward to the target. The haul is made in a direction back and down. The rod hand and the line hand move opposite each other during the haul, but it is the line hand, which pulls away from the rod hand. The rod hand will travel in its usual path, as it does when there is no haul. When your thumb is positioned 90 ° to the target, and you are ready

Photo series 21- top:- forward cast start position; bottom: haul is opposite rod direction

to stop the rod, the line hand accelerates away from the rod hand, while the rod hand continues its path to a stop. This pulling of the line hand away from the rod hand increases the tension in the fly casting system and increases the loading of the rod. When learning the haul, you should focus on adding your line hand, not changing your rod hand.

The give back is the return of the line, which you have just hauled. At the end of the haul, the line hand pauses for a moment. This allows the rod tip to move from bent to straight, and form the loop. It is the energy in the loop of line, which will take back the line from your line hand. This is an important concept. After you haul, if you intend to give the line back, you must wait for a moment for the loop to form. When you give back the line, you must give it back slowly. The haul is sharp, but the give back portion is slow. You will give the line back, in a direction that moves your line hand back toward your rod hand. The line hand should stop a little lower than your rod hand so the line does not get tangled on the reel handle.

The speed that you give back line will be determined by the speed of the unrolling loop of line. You can only give back the line at the speed that the unrolling loop can accept it. The speed of the give back must match the speed of the unrolling loop. While holding the line securely in your line hand fingers, relax your hand and arm. You must feel for the loop of line gently pulling the fly line from your line hand. You can watch the piece of line from the first stripping guide to your line hand. Give the line back only at a speed which maintains tension on this section of line (just like when false casting). If you give the line back too quickly, you will see slack in the section of line. If you give back too slowly, tension is maintained but not all the line is returned and you must now hold that line for the remainder of the cast.

The single haul is a one-direction move, it is a haul without a give back. Some people find this easier to learn. The single haul can be used on a back cast, a forward cast, or both. The key feature is that you do not give the line back after the haul. A single haul on the back cast is generally used when casting into a tailwind, and the wind prevents your giving back the line. The loop unrolling into the wind does not have sufficient speed to accept the give back of the line without creating slack. In this situation, you get the benefit of increased load, and higher line speed of the haul. You do not give back line to ensure the system stays under tension, without slack. A single haul on the forward cast can be helpful when casting into a strong headwind, or anytime you want higher line speed on the delivery cast. If you have a strong tailwind and still want the forward cast delivery at high speed, this is when to use two single hauls.

For a single haul, the haul is executed in the same way as with a double haul. The haul occurs in coordination with the stop. It is matched to the cast for acceleration and the stop for length. The haul is sharp and ends abruptly. It occurs in a direction opposite the rod hand. In the single haul, the line hand maintains its position after the stop of the haul.

When using a single haul be sure to end the haul with a bend in your line hand elbow. The forearm is not at full extension. When you perform a single haul on the back cast, be aware of the position of your line hand after the stop. The line hand must pivot to maintain its position relative to the rod hand, as your rod hand moves forward for the forward cast. The line hand maintains this position throughout the cast and can shoot the line on delivery or can simply hold onto the line. On the forward cast single haul, the line hand will haul with your rod hand wrist rotation on the stop. After the stop, the line hand holds its position. You can then hold the line or release it for shooting. If you release the line, it is not a give back, but a shoot.

You can also use two single hauls. You can use a single haul on the back cast and another single haul on the forward cast. After the back cast, your line hand maintains its hauled position. During the forward cast the line hand pivots to maintain its position relative to the rod hand. When the rod hand is positioned for the stop, the line hand has pivoted. It has maintained its position relative to the rod hand. Now make another single haul on the forward cast. Your line hand will now be at full extension. Deciding whether to use a single or double haul will be dictated by the situation. Be prepared to do both, and you will be well equipped.

To learn the hauls you can start with either single or the double haul. Most people find the two-direction move of the double haul to be challenging. If this is your situation, start with the single hauls and when ready you can move to the double haul.

Learning to single haul

To learn the single haul, start with a single haul on the back cast. Have your line straight on the water in front of you. Move your line hand and rod hand in the same direction to start the casting stroke. When you reach the line leader connection, the rod hand will execute the wrist rotation for the stop, while the line hand accelerates in an opposite direction for the haul. Be sure to stop the line hand haul when the rod hand stops. As you lift the line off the water, if your rod hand is relaxed, you can feel the rod bending. The haul should feel like you are pulling into this bend, creating a deeper bend. Think of the back cast haul as helping to lift the fly off the water. Within the casting stroke, the loading move is the longest part. The stop and haul are relatively short in comparison.

The wrist rotation and haul are very brief; they last just long enough to lift the fly off the water. When the fly leaves the water, your haul is complete and the rod is stopped. Your rod hand maintains its position while the loop unrolls. On the next forward cast, pivot your line hand to maintain its position relative to the rod hand and holding the line firmly throughout the forward cast, follow through and then present the fly.

Photo series 22- L-single haul on back cast, note line hand positions and bend in elbow at end of haul,; R- haul arm pivots on forward cast

To make a single haul on the forward cast, make a back cast as usual. The forward cast will start the same as all forward casts. The haul will be added toward the end of the casting stroke when you have reached the stop position. Move your rod arm and line hand forward during the loading move. Align your thumb with the target. When your thumb is directly opposite the target, the rod hand starts its wrist rotation to a stop. Your line hand starts the acceleration of the haul. The haul is opposite the rod hand. The line hand travels down and back toward your left hip. After the stop, you can hold the line or release it for shooting.

Photo series 23- L- forward cast single haul, hands start in same direction; R- separate on the stop

Now try a single haul on the back cast followed by a single haul on the forward cast. Remember that as you start the forward casting stroke, the line hand must pivot to maintain its position relative to the rod hand. If you have stopped your back cast haul with your elbow bent, you will be able to add a second single haul on the forward cast. This is a technique for presentation, not for false casting.

Learning to double haul

Even when you understand the movements of the double haul, it is not always easy to execute. When learning the double haul, spend a few minutes pantomiming the movements before using your rod. Use just your hands and focus on the movement of both hands. Note the timing, direction and speed of both the haul and the give back.

Focus on hauling

You can use a technique that allows you to focus on the haul movements without using your rod arm, and is practiced on a field. Place two targets on the ground approximately 40 feet apart. Use approximately 30 feet of line and place the rod butt in your rod armpit. Next, wrap your rod arm under and around the rod shaft. Reach up, and grip the rod with your rod hand fingers. You will false cast the line in the horizontal pane. Use your body and swing the rod from side to side to form a casting loop. Your body provides line speed and the stops. Watch your loops. They should unroll in line with your targets. When the loops look good, add your line hand and begin to haul. Your hauls are coordinated with the stops and occur in an opposite direction to the rod movement. In the horizontal plane, the back cast haul moves to your left. The forward cast haul is back, toward your left hip. Focus on the haul and give back. Be sure to avoid slack line from your rod hand to the first stripping guide. Make multiple false casts in this position, focusing on the haul and give back while being smooth with your line hand.

Photo series 24- top: rod secured; L use body to swing rod and make stops; R- haul with line hand-

Horizontal double haul

You can learn the double haul by casting in the horizontal position on grass. This is my favorite technique as it allows you to move slowly through the casting stroke and see the cast as it is occurs. You can see all the parts of the cast: the loading of the rod and the positioning for the stop, the effect of your haul and give back and your accuracy to the targets.

Using 40 feet of fly line, place your rod on the ground and straighten your fly line so it is at a right angle to the rod. Place a target down at the end of your leader. Walk the fly line to the other direction. When you have the line straight off the rod tip, put the second target down. Now you have a target for your back cast and forward cast.

Stand facing the middle. You have one target to your right, the

Photo 32-horizontal casting set-up

other to your left. Hold your rod in your rod hand with the line trapped under your middle finger. Rotate your hand and forearm so your palm is up toward the sky. Your forearm should feel like you could slide your forearm sideways across a tabletop. Start by making a back cast and let it fall. You can see if you are in line with your target. Next, make a forward cast, again check for accuracy. Practice false casting in this horizontal position to be comfortable with the set up, before adding the double haul. When you are comfortable, you can add your line hand.

Slowly make a back cast and haul. Give the line back and allow the loop to fall. Focus on the line hand and rod hand starting the casting stroke together and separating on the stop. In this position, you can watch your hands move. Be sure they start moving in the same direction. Remember that, the moving of the rod to get it loaded is the longest part of the casting stroke; the stop and haul are relatively short and occur at the end of the stroke.

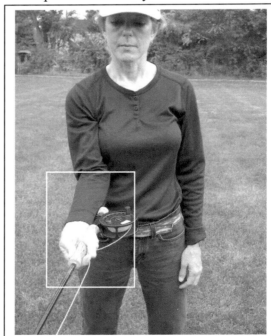

Photo 33-palm and forearm rotate to horizontal position

You will see the rod tip bend as it starts to load. You will also see how the haul affects the cast. You can watch your line hand to be sure it hauls in concert with the rod hand stop and then maintains the line under tension during the give back move. As always, be sure your casting stroke is in line with your target.

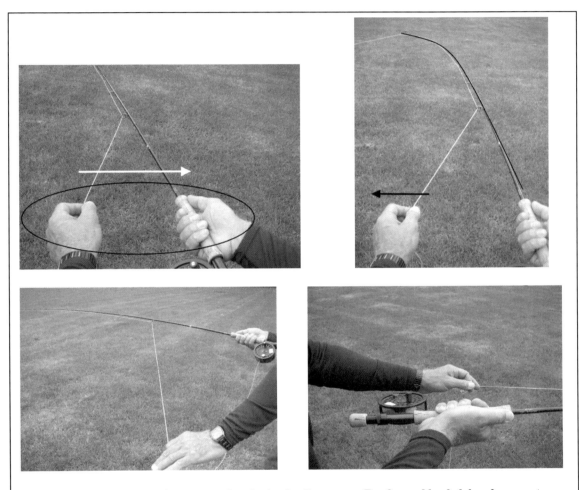

Photo series 25 top: L- hands start together during loading move,; R- after rod loaded, hands separate on the stop; bottom L - line hand hauls opposite the rod hand; R- give back line as loop unrolls

Now you are ready for a forward cast and haul. Be sure your hands start the casting stroke by moving in the same direction during the loading move. The haul occurs with the stop and is directed toward your left hip. Watch your line during the give back and be sure there is no slack. Allow the loop to unroll. Stop and evaluate your cast and double haul.

Photo series 26- top L- looking forward, hands start in same direction for loading move; R- rod bent before the haul ; bottom: line hand hauls down toward left hip

When casting in this position your back cast haul will be opposite the rod. In the horizontal position, the rod hand moves to the right so the haul will be to the left. On the forward cast, the rod is moving forward, so the haul is directed back, toward your left hip. The beauty of this exercise is that you can practice one cast and double haul at a time. You can move slowly and deliberately though each cast. You have time to analyze each cast. When you feel confident with your haul and give back, you can false cast with the double haul in the horizontal position. You can watch the entire cast and double haul sequence. This position fatigues your rod arm, so only make a few casts then rest your arm before starting again. Remember to relax your hand for fresh hand strength and tension on the stops. Once you feel comfortable with the double haul in the horizontal position, move to the off vertical position and false cast. This is a comfortable position for many casters.

Hauls in the vertical plane

Hauls can also be performed while casting in the vertical and off shoulder stances. The mechanics of the haul remain the same. The direction of the haul changes, because the casting plane has changed. When casting in a vertical plane, closed stance, the back cast rod movement is directed back and up. The haul will be forward and down. The line hand haul ends almost over your right foot. The forward cast rod direction is down and forward. The haul movement is down and back, toward your left knee or hip (same haul positions as for single hauls).

In the off shoulder stance, the rod still moves back and up, with the rod over your left shoulder. The haul will again be down and forward. The haul is toward the inside of your right foot. On the forward cast the rod is moving down and out, your haul will again be down and back, this time toward the outside of your left foot.

Hauls:
- Haul is an acceleration to a stop
- Occurs with the wrist rotation on the stop
- Are matched to the rod hand acceleration and length of the stop
- Made in a direction opposite the movement of the rod hand
- Haul is sharp
- Give back is slow
- Give back speed is matched to the rate of the unrolling loop

Photo series 27- top: back cast haul directed forward and down; mid: line hand returns to rod hand; bottom: forward cast haul, down and back

Shooting Line more Efficiently

Line can be shot after the stop on either the back cast or the forward cast. When the rod stops and the loop is formed, the energy from the loaded rod is unloaded into the loop. The loop has energy that can be used to shoot line. How much line you can shoot is determined by several factors. The amount of fly line you are casting and its weight will affect how much line you can shoot. Because the line is weight, you must have a sufficient amount of fly line weight outside the rod tip to be able to shoot line. Use caution with simply false casting more fly line. You must be able to carry the line you are casting smoothly in the air. You need the correct speed, power, the proper stroke length and casting arc or you will have slack line and no energy for a line shoot. The amount of load in the rod must be sufficient to have energy available to form the loop and pull additional line for a shoot. You also need an abrupt stop to transfer the energy from the rod to the fly line.

Fly line design affects how much line you can shoot. The weighted section of your fly line is the maximum amount of line to false cast. With the weighted section near the rod tip, you maximize the fly line design by having the weighted section pull the un-weighted running line behind it as the loop unrolls. A weight forward, triangle taper or shooting head line design are some of the more common designs which are easier for shooting line. A level or double taper fly line has a long continuous belly, which makes it great for long roll casts, but very difficult to shoot distance.

The maximum amount of line to false cast is the entire head length. When you shoot line beyond the head, you are adding thinner diameter running line. Because it is thinner, it does not have enough mass to help the loop unroll, or change direction for the next cast. This makes it difficult to control the cast. If you have shot too much line and false cast with the head far from the rod tip, you will likely lose control of the cast. Therefore, the fly line design limits the amount of line you can false cast.

Overhang refers to how far away from the rod tip the weighted section of line is located. If the weighted section is close to the rod tip, the line is easier to control. As the weighted section gets further away from the rod tip, you get a hinging effect. It is more difficult to control the line. The running line does not have enough mass to help control the weighted section. The result is an out of control loop. This is common with casters randomly shooting line while false casting. They overshoot line until they can no longer control the cast. To avoid this situation, know the head length of your fly line. Your maximum false cast should be the head length plus a small amount of overhang. This allows you to keep the fly line in control, and maintain an energy efficient loop. You can shoot more line on your delivery cast, but keep the false casts in control.

Line can be shot after the stop on either the back cast or the forward cast. Once you have stopped the rod and the loop forms, there is energy in that loop to be able to shoot line. Shooting line on multiple false casts requires the ability to control the shoot. Your line hand must release line on the shoot and then re-secure the line after the shoot. This allows another cast to be made. When you can successfully release and re-trap the line, you can add the technique of shooting line on your back cast. By shooting line on your back cast, you can minimize your false casting. You now have two opportunities to shoot line, on both the back cast and the forward cast.

Start with shooting a foot of line on the back cast. Make a forward cast and shoot another foot of line. Again, re-trap the line. Make a second back cast and shoot an additional foot of line. Then make your delivery cast and shoot as much line as you can.

As you develop your ability to control the shoot and re-trap of line, you should strive for making as few false casts as possible. Once you are casting the entire head of the fly line, you should shoot only on the final back cast, the one before you plan to deliver the fly. If you continue false casting and shooting line, you will exceed your abilities to handle overhang, and the cast suffers. Your plan for efficiency should be to false cast the weighted section of line, shoot a small amount of line on the forward cast and final back cast. Then shoot the remaining line on the next forward casts delivery.

Efficient Shooting Line:
- False cast longer line, for more weight for longer shoot
- Maximum length to false cast is the head of the fly line
- Minimize overhang
- Shoot line on forward cast and last back cast
- Train line hand to alternately pinch and release line for controlled shoot

Increasing Distance

Stroke Length

Most anglers want the ability to cast further. They feel t
a few feet beyond where they can cast. As a beginner, forty feet
intermediate caster you are likely seeking to be consistent and re
more feet. To cast more distance you will need to apply a few ba
sure to maintain the fundamentals of a good efficient cast.

To cast more distance you need a deeper bend or load in   ....used load
will give you more energy to transfer to the fly line. This gives you more loop speed to shoot

more line, yielding a longer casting range. As
always, this must be accomplished while casting
in a straight line, applying power smoothly and
avoiding slack line.

A longer cast requires a longer casting
stroke. If you accelerate the rod over a longer
distance, you smoothly create more bend in the
rod and more energy for the cast. Stroke length is
the distance your hand and arm move during the
cast. Your natural maximum stroke length is the
distance your forearm moves. From your
forearm extended, to when your forearm hits
your upper arm and your arm has run out of
room to move.

**Photo 34- maximum stroke length limited
by body**

To increase stroke length, start by adding body movement. While making the back

cast pick up, bend your
knees and lean forward.
This increases your stroke
length by a few inches.
After the stop, slide back
slightly to get another
inch of stroke length.
When leaning back, be
sure to move horizontally,
not downward, to
maintain a straight line.
Body movement with
weight shifting smoothly
adds a few inches to your
stroke length. If you need
additional stroke length,

Photo series 28- longer stroke length with body movement

you can use the off vertical casting plane with an open stance and add something called drift.

Off Vertical-Open Stance

Many anglers, especially in saltwater find it easier to use on open stance and cast in the off vertical plane while adding body movement to the cast. In this stance, your rod hand side foot is dropped back and outward for a wider base. Your hips and shoulders are rotated so they are at a slight angle to the target. Your forearm is tilted slight out away from your body, but your elbow remains fairly close to your side.

With this position, it is easy to use an off vertical casting plane. The off vertical means that you are no longer casting right in line with your body (forearm in front of your shoulder and upper arm). You are off to the side. Your elbow remains close to your body. Your forearm and hand tilt out from your body, similar to your roll cast position. You can cast at any angle from horizontal to slightly off vertical. When starting with the off vertical position, use a 20-30° angle to be sure you maintain your body alignment for a straight cast.

Photo 35-- off vertical position

In the off vertical stance, it is easy to let your elbow move away from your side. This makes it more difficult to get a good abrupt back cast stop directly opposite your target. When you stop the rod on the back cast, your hand should stop in front of your shoulder. Your forearm will hit the lower portion of your bicep muscle. The structure of your forearm and hand help you stop the rod. Joan Wulff calls this a body block. This body block creates a definitive stop point for you. When you feel your forearm touch your upper arm, the stroke should end. Having this definitive stop point helps you to accelerate right up to the stop. The body block is your built in tool to get a good stop even with a longer stroke.

Photo 36- body block, elbow close to side

Body Rotation

To maximize the open stance and off vertical position you can add a body rotation during the casting stroke. This body rotation helps you smoothly accelerate through the stroke and helps you with the abrupt stop. As you start the back cast from the open stance, your shoulders are tilted just slightly away from the target. Start by rotating your hand and forearm while you lift the line. Your hand and forearm rotate to accommodate a straight line path of the rod. After your hand and forearm rotate, continue to accelerate the rod to the stop position. The stop position will be when your forearm and upper arm meet and your hand is in line with your shoulders. As your forearm and hand accelerate through the stroke, your hips and shoulders also rotate. They rotate to allow the forearm to move in a straight line path. Joan Wulff calls this a body snap. When you end the casting stroke, your shoulders and hips have rotated to be approximately 90° to the target. Your elbow is still relatively close to your side and your hand has stopped in front of your shoulder. The rotation of your shoulders and hips is not done forcefully, but can have a speed or quickness to it. The rotation is small, almost a quarter turn. When the rotation is complete, you stop the rod. The body snap helps the abrupt stop because your entire body is suddenly stopping when your hips rotate from a 45° to a 90° angle to the target. From this position, you can more easily add drift.

Photo series 29- L- open stance start position, R- body rotation: hips & shoulder rotate

Drift

Drift is a repositioning of the rod tip after the stop. You can reposition in any direction while the cast unrolls during drift time. Typically, drift refers to repositioning the rod tip backward. For distance casting, you will want to reposition the rod tip backward for a longer forward casting stroke. This repositioning occurs along the same straight line, which you have made your cast. The drift is an extension of this straight line trajectory. Drift occurs without power. It is a relaxed effortless motion.

Photo series 30- L-stop position; R- repositioning of rod with drift

In the vertical position, the drift is back and up. After you stop the rod, you drift up. Notice your elbow lifting. The forward casting stroke can now be longer because you have repositioned the rod tip further back with drift. Drift is useful because it allows for a longer casting stroke. This allows you to build more load in the rod. Drift also keeps you in contact with your line as it unrolls off the rod tip. Rather than the downtime while waiting for the loop to unroll, drift makes your casting motion more fluid. It fills this gap with a constant feeling of tension on your rod tip.

Photo series 31- L- stop in vertical plane; R- vertical drift, up and back

In the off vertical position, drift also continues the straight line of the cast. Drift will be in the same plane. In the off vertical plane, the drift trajectory feels flatter because your cast is on a shallow trajectory. In the off vertical plane, the direction of the drift is back and out. Your elbow leaves you side as you reach back to reposition the rod tip in the direction of your loop.

Photo series 32-L- elbow close to side on stop; R- elbow leaves side on drift

Start with short drifts of only a few inches. As this becomes more natural, you can add more drift. Remember it is crucial to make the abrupt stop first, and then the drift. If you run the stop and drift together, you are likely to come off the straight line for your cast. Stop first, and then drift. To make your next forward cast, start by moving your elbow back to its original position on the stop. I think of this as a recollecting yourself to your stop position. With your elbow back by your side, you can continue the forward cast as usual.

Distance Casting:
- Increase stroke length and casting arc
- Use off vertical and open stance position
- Body rotation to facilitate straight line path of rod
- Drift after back cast stop for longer forward casting stroke

Additional Distance Adjustments:

Timing

Once you have increased the stroke length and are casting longer lines, you need to adjust your timing. A longer cast with a longer loop takes more time to unroll. The pause after the stop is longer. You will need to develop a sense of timing for this longer cast. When casting off vertical with an open stance, you can turn your head to watch the back cast unroll. Watch for the loop to be almost fully unrolled. When the loop resembles a sideways candy cane and a few feet of line and leader are yet to unroll, this is your cue to gradually start the next cast. This visual, will help with your timing. Be sure to turn your head only. If you turn your shoulders or arm, you will come off the straight line path of your cast. When you see the loop has almost unrolled, turn your head back to aim your forward cast and begin your forward casting stroke.

Acceleration

When casting longer lines, the acceleration needs to increase. The rate of acceleration to cast 40 ft will be greater than the acceleration needed to cast 20 feet. You will also need a slightly higher line speed to keep the longer cast aloft and fight gravity. You do not need to move at top speed. Use just the amount of acceleration needed and no excess as it will detract from your cast.

Trajectory

Trajectory refers to the angle of the cast. The most efficient fly casting occurs on a straight line. The straight line is on some angle both away from and toward your target. The long length of line and distant target requires a more shallow the trajectory. It is almost perpendicular to the ground. For very long casts, your back cast trajectory will be at the horizon behind you. The forward cast trajectory will be at or just above the horizon in front. Be sure to adjust your trajectory when casting distance so your loop has time to unroll.

Casting Arc

When casting distance you will need a wider casting arc to accommodate the deeper bend in the rod. The wider arc allows the rod tip to travel in a straight line path. Be sure to watch your rod shaft as you cast to ensure you are using a wider casting arc. The wider casting arc will be oriented perpendicular to the ground to allow for the shallower trajectory.

Photo series 33- L- flat trajectory for long cast; R- wider arc for deeper load

To increase your casting distance you will need to combine the techniques of longer casting strokes, wider arc, add the double haul and your principles about shooting line efficiently. Your increased distance will not occur overnight. It will be a gradually increase, as you improve your techniques, the extra distance will come.

Summary:

Intermediate casting focuses on improving your range of skills and improving your ability to handle more difficult, fishing situations. You must maintain the fundamental casting principles, as you develop your style of casting. As your fundamentals improve, you can add the double and single haul techniques and utilize style adjustments to help increase casting distance.

Just as when you were a beginner, you will only get your casting skills to the next level if you practice. At this point in your casting, you should practice on a field. The water will only distract you and make you want to fish. Practice time and fishing time should be separate. This is how you will get the most from your practice time. Your practice will pay off in your fishing, when your new skills are ingrained in your body and mind. Use the guide for intermediate casting techniques in the practice section of this book.

Intermediate Casting:
- Five essentials for all casts
- Casting in the wind
- Hauls: double and single
- Efficient shooting line
- Beginning distance casting

Fishing Situations & Applications

Many people start their fishing in saltwater and experienced freshwater fisherman may expand to the salt. If you fish in the northeast and fish for stripers, bluefish and false albacore, you should know how to fish a sinking line, and be able to use the oval cast.

Oval cast

An oval cast is used when casting heavy flies, using sinking lines, or when you do not have enough space for a straight line back cast. It is particularly helpful for striper fisherman when casting the sinking lines or heavy Clouser flies to handle the extra weight. The oval cast allows the line and fly to unroll behind you in a curve fashion. This curved motion allows the line and fly to make a more gradual transition from the back cast to the forward cast. The weight from a heavy fly or a sinking line can "kick" when the line unrolls. This destroys the smooth nature of the casting stroke. The oval cast is made by using a shallow dip or curved motion when you make the wrist rotation for the back cast stop. The curving motion makes the line and fly ride upward and in a small circular movement. When the line has almost unrolled, start the forward cast as usual.

Sinking Lines

The key to using sinking lines is to remember the line has two parts. The head section, which is the weighted section and the running line, is un-weighted. Work with the entire head of the shooting line at the rod tip. False cast only the head of the fly line and use the running line for shooting to your distance. Use your roll cast to straighten the line on the surface of the water. As soon as the line is straight on the surface, start your back cast. Using the double haul, make the back cast and shoot some line. Next make your forward cast and shoot the rest of your line. When fishing with shooting lines keep your false casting to a minimum. After stripping the line all the way in, you will need to recast. Wiggle the head of the line outside the rod tip, just like when you started fishing. Roll cast the line to straighten it and raise it to the surface, then start your casting sequence again.

River Fishing for the intermediate caster

The specialty casts and nuances involved in fishing a river can take a lifetime to fine tune. There are volumes written on presentation casts. This section is not the entire compendium of presentation options. This represents the most common presentations casts that all river anglers should master.

Mends

When fishing in a river, you must be able to mend your fly line for a natural presentation of your fly. A mend is a repositioning of the fly line in order to get a longer drag free drift. You can make an on the water mend. You learned this mend as a beginner. The line lands on the water and you make an adjustment after it lands to reposition the line upstream. You can also make an in the air mend (aerial mend). This is a mend where the line is repositioned before it lands on the water. It is more advanced because you are anticipating the need for the drift. You are proactively managing your fly line. To make aerial mends you need to find follow through time. Normally, after you stop the rod, you follow through with the rod tip down to the water. When making an aerial mend, you will use follow through time to adjust the fly line while also lowering the rod tip. The classic in the air mend is a reach cast.

The reach is made by reaching your rod to the right or left while the loop is unrolling. Make the cast toward the target. As the cast is unrolling move your rod arm (right or left) upstream so the fly line is placed upstream of the fly. The reach is done without power. It is a gentle repositioning of the rod after the stop. The reach can be upstream or downstream depending on your need to slow down or speed up your fly's drift.

When you use the reach cast, the fly may land short of your target. This is because you have originally measured the casting distance for a straight line delivery. When making your mend with the reach, you have lengthened the distance between your rod tip and the target. To adjust for this change in distance, pull extra line off the reel. During the reach, allow this line to be pulled out during the cast. This is called slipping line. Slipping line with the reach cast will allow you to reach your target and have a longer drag free drift.

Once you have mastered the reach cast both right and left, you are ready to understand more about mends. Mends can be made in different places in your fly line, in varying directions, and in varying shapes. To make a mend, move the rod in a direction after the stop. To make a mend to the right, move the rod horizontally to the right. To make a mend to the left, move the rod to the left. You move the rod in the direction, then return it to midline (the position of your stop). To make the mend a deep or wider mend, move the rod further over in the horizontal direction. If you want the mend to be longer, hold the rod in position of the mend a little longer before returning to midline. Now you can make a shallow or deep mend and can make it longer or shorter.

Where in the fly line you place the mend is determined by how soon after the stop you move the rod to make the mend. To make a mend near the tip of the fly line, make the mend very soon after the stop. For a mend in the middle of the line, pause for a moment after the stop, then make the mend. To place the mend close to you, near the end of the line, after the stop, watch your line unroll. Make your mend just before the line falls to the water. You can also make more than one mend. To make a series of mends, you can wiggle the rod side to side for the duration of the follow through time. This results in the classic serpentine or wiggle cast.

Slack Line casts

You can introduce slack line to create a longer drag free drift. The pile cast is a cast that puts a lot of slack in your line, near the fly. To make the pile cast, on your last false cast allow the back cast to unroll and fall a little. Aim the forward cast very high perhaps at a cloud or tree top. After the stop, lower your rod tip quickly. Your fly and leader will land in a puddle of line allowing lots of downstream drag free drift. If you want slack line closer toward you, make your cast as usual, but delay your follow through until the fly touches the water. Now lower your rod tip and you will have lots of slack line near you to feed into the cast for a longer drift.

Curve Casts

The curve cast is another tool for the river fisherman. The curve casts help you place the fly around an object. Curve casts are known by many names and can be made by different maneuvers. The most popular curve casts are the overpowered and underpowered curve casts. The underpowered curve is a cast in which the loop does not completely unroll. It slows down gradually and has a soft stop. In the vertical plane, this underpowered cast can be executed by drawing the shape of a question mark (?) in the air. You move your rod around the object. The cast falls softly, around your object. After this cast you frequently need an on the water mend to adjust your drag free drift.

The overpowered curve cast is used more often because it allows more control over the final placement of the fly. Cast in the horizontal plane, being sure to cast in a straight line. On your final delivery cast, make your cast with extra power. The loop unrolls fully with extra energy. This extra energy causes and the fly to bounce around to the side, (right-handed cast, the fly bounces to the left) making the curve.

Change of Direction

When fishing in a river you will need to change direction frequently. Most often, you change direction from a downstream position to an upstream position. As a beginner, you change directions by false casting, making small degrees of change with each new false cast. As an experienced caster, you will want to accomplish the change of direction with fewer false casts allowing more time with your fly in the water. There are numerous options available to change direction. The particular fishing situation will dictate which will work best. I will present several options. You should practice and try them all and use the option which best fits the situation.

Using a clock face as your reference, if the fly is in a downstream position at 2 o'clock, make a back cast. While the cast is unrolling, rotate your body to an upstream position of 11 o'clock and present the fly. This takes one cast and you are back fishing. You can use this same technique to move from your left to your right. In this case, you make an off shoulder back cast. While the back cast is unrolling, turn to your right and present the fly. This works well if fishing with the stream running right to left.

You can use this same principle with a rotation of your arm. Make a back cast from your right side. While the cast is unrolling, rotate your rod arm to the off shoulder position. The presentation is on your left, with an off shoulder forward cast. You can also rotate from off shoulder to dominant shoulder. You have two rotation options. In the first case, you rotate your torso similar to a body rotation. In the second situation, you rotate your rod arm similar to the casting in all planes.

If you have a large angle of change from 3 o'clock position to 9 o'clock position, you will want to add an additional false cast. In this situation, make a back cast from 3 o'clock position, rotate your body and face the 12 o'clock position while your back cast unrolls. Now make a forward cast (false cast). Make another back cast. While this is unrolling, again rotate your body and face the 3 o'clock position. Now make your presentation cast. You have accomplished a 180° angle of change with only two false casts.

You can also change from a straight downstream position (fly on the dangle) to a straight upstream position with one cast. Allow your fly to be pulled straight downstream. Turn and face upstream and raise your rod up beside you. You are in your normal position for the end of the back cast. When your fly line is tight, and you have no slack line, make a forward cast directly upstream. This cast usually has a wider loop because the line as started behind you down on the water. The wider loop makes this a great option for heavy flies or a two fly outfit.

Fishing Adaptations: recognizing and adjusting the parts of the cast

As an intermediate caster you should be able to identify the different parts of the casting stroke (loading move, wrist rotation on the stop, follow through and drift). Once you identify the parts, you can vary them to get different outcomes, which can help you in fishing.

The loading move is typically done by moving the rod arm in a straight line. There are times you may want to vary this. On the back cast, you have many options for lifting your line off the water. Rather than a straight line, you can choose to move your hand and rod in a circular fashion while lifting the line. This helps your line and fly lift off the water with very little water disturbance. Start with your rod tip low to the water. During the lift, and while you are accelerating, move your rod hand in a large circle. Be sure to stop in an upward motion, in the usual back cast stop position. Make your forward cast as usual. You can also move the rod in a vertical direction. This is the jump pick up. During the lift of the line off the water, move your rod hand up and down a few times. This will cause the fly line to jump up, off the water. This can also be used with horizontal movement of the rod on the pickup. This is helpful if there is debris on the water, and you need to shake it off your line during the pickup. The important concept is to be sure you stop with the rod moving up into your usual back cast stop position. This positions the line so the back cast will unroll normally, followed by a typical forward cast.

You can modify your wrist rotation. You can vary the direction or power of the wrist rotation. On the back cast, a curving wrist rotation is the foundation of the Oval cast. Make an off vertical back cast that allows the hand to move in a shallow dip or curve, rising up on the stop. On the back cast, this curving wrist movement causes the line and fly pass under the rod tip and, unroll in an upward direction. This is useful with heavy flies or sinking lines. On your forward cast, you can make a curving wrist rotation. This gives you a curve for your delivery cast, to place the line around an obstacle. This is done by making your hand rotate in a quick, twisting motion during the wrist rotation part of the cast. Lastly, you can adjust the power in your wrist rotation. On the forward cast, you can apply extra power to make your cast unroll with excess force. This causes the fly to bounce back at you. In the vertical plane, this is the Tuck cast, in the horizontal plane it is a curve cast.

Follow through time can also be varied by direction or timing. After the forward cast stop and the loop is unrolling, you can move the rod sideways to reposition the line upstream or downstream to vary the fly's drift, for a reach cast. When you vary, the timing of your follow through, it affects the slack line in your cast. If you follow through quickly with the rod tip, you will have slack out at the leader and tip of the fly line. If your delay your follow through until after the cast has touched the water, and then lower your rod tip, you will have slack near the rod tip.

You should practice all of these techniques, and discover how varying the parts of the cast can help you in your fishing.

Lesson 3: Distance Casting

Most fly fisherman hold distance casting as a measure of their skill. For this lesson, distance casting is concerned with casts of 75 feet or more. In order to cast distance you must be capable of executing the fundamentals correctly, or there will be no distance. Distance casting magnifies any small flaw in your cast. For instance, a one-degree error in accuracy transmitted 90 feet away can yield a fly placement that is several feet off target. Any imperfection in your basic casting mechanics will impede your distance casting. The greater the distance, the more important each detail of the cast becomes. This is the reason distance casting is one measure of your abilities as a fly caster. You may also be seeking distance not just as a measure of skill, but for practical purposes. You may want to improve your fishing ability, reaching fish further away, or more time for your fly in the water. If your best cast is 50 feet and the wind picks up, your casting distance will probably decrease to 40 feet. However, if you can cast 80 feet, and you have a stiff breeze, you are likely to execute a 65-70 foot cast. This ability to more effectively fish in adverse conditions is the most important reason to improve your distance casting. Do not use distance casting to throw your mistakes farther. Casting a long line that ends in a mess does not help you. You need a long cast that presents well and is reproducible. By developing your fundamentals and improving your efficiency, your distance will be solid and a thing of beauty.

Most anglers look for new techniques, to help them cast more distance. Once you have increased your stroke length, added the double haul and shooting line, there are very few new techniques to add. The majority of your improvement as a distance caster will come from refining your fundamental casting mechanics and improving your efficiency. You must be willing to make changes in these areas in order to increase your distance.

All anglers develop habits. Some habits may only be problematic as they seek more distance. At this point, these habits become a liability and a change is in order. You can cast in any style you like. When this style no longer helps, you will need to change. Achieving your ultimate distance cast will likely involve some changes in style, as well as refining your fundamental casting mechanics. A style change can help you perform the casting mechanics to the greater efficiency required for distance casting. It is always surprising when a small modification results in major benefits. When casting distance a small change is magnified over a large area so the effect can be great. Never underestimate the ability of a small change in yourself to yield great outcomes in your cast.

As you strive for distance, you will need to improve your efficiency for each cast. Distance casting is about focusing on the details of each cast and perfecting your execution of the details. To improve efficiency you will need to develop a greater range of your skills. Most casters have one cast. They have one speed and one style, which they apply in all situations. As you improve your casting, you will develop a range of stroke lengths, rates of acceleration, and amount of power in the stop. You will learn to match your line hand functions with your rod hand functions throughout this range. All casting is about energy in the cast. The goal is to match the energy required with the situation, in order to have the perfect cast. You also want a cast that is reproducible, which you can perform all day long.

Efficient Loading and Unloading the fly rod

Loading the fly rod means bending the rod. The ability to make a cast relies on the interaction between your fly rod and the fly line. The fly rod can bend and straighten. The fly line provides weight for the rod to bend. The flexible weight can form a loop with energy. This loop unrolls and delivers the fly to your target. The interaction between rod and line is what we anglers try to maximize. The angler is the primary mediator between the rod and the line. You need to maximize your role to create the perfect cast.

Every fly rod wants something different. The ultimate distance and maximum efficiency is about finding the right balance for each rod. This balance is between the rod's action, the fly line's design, and your individual ability for power, speed, timing and smoothness. The fly rod bends as it moves against the weight and resistance of the fly line. The deeper the bend in the rod, the more spring flex action the rod can impart to the cast. A longer cast requires a deeper load so more energy can be transferred to the line. This yields higher line speed and the ability for the cast to travel further.

When casting distance you need to maximize your ability to load and unload the rod. Efficiency in your cast means no wasted movement. Every inch of movement should contribute to the cast. To improve your efficiency and focus on the details of casting fundamentals, start by isolating each cast. Focus on just the back cast and then just the forward cast. This will help to develop your rod arm mechanics. Start by using just your rod arm with the line trapped under your grip. Add your line hand after your rod arm mechanics have improved and you are ready to focus on the hauls.

Back Cast Loading

The back cast is the set up for your forward cast. Rarely does a good forward cast occur after a bad back cast. A good back cast is the perfect set up and enhances the probability of a good forward cast. To improve you must remove yourself from the distraction of fish. You already know the feeling of lifting line off the water, so begin your practice and on a grass field. By casting on grass, you are better able to focus on skill building. After you practice on grass, move to the water and try to recreate your new skills. Initially, the practice casting feels different from the casting while fishing. Eventually, the casting skills from practice will cross over and the casting while fishing will improve.

Start with the line straight in front of you to eliminate slack. Place your rod tip low to the grass. This is your starting position. From this position, the rod will start loading immediately when you move the rod. For rod loading to begin immediately two factors must occur: you must have no slack line and you must start with the rod tip low. This position keeps the fly line under tension and helps you efficiently load the rod.

Photo series 34-top: rod tip low allows rod to bend early in stroke, maximizes efficiency; bottom: - rod tip high creates slack line, not efficient loading (slack seen when rod tip lowered)

Begin with the vertical position, your shoulders square to the target. This keeps your forearm in line with your upper arm. This position helps you move the rod in a straight line, which is crucial to efficient casting. Use the thumb on top grip. Your wrist is in the bent down position, and your rod butt is in line with the underside of your forearm. You should have a relaxed hand. As you start the back cast, imagine the trajectory as being back and up. Pretend you are trying to make your cast unroll over a fence behind you.

To lift the line, use your entire forearm and hand as a unit. If you lift with just your hand, you are likely to move in a curved pattern, which is inefficient. Lift your forearm and rod butt together. Move on an upward diagonal path stopping your hand near your temple. In this path, you will see and feel your elbow rise. This ensures an upward as well as backward trajectory of the cast. During the lift, your wrist stays in the bent down position and the rod butt stays in line with your forearm.

Lift with just enough acceleration to move the line. Continue lifting until you reach the line leader connection. When the line leader connection begins to lift, the stroke ends with the abrupt stop.

The abrupt stop transfers the energy from the rod to the fly line and is crucial to getting energy into the line. To stop the rod squeeze your rod hand tightly, while also tightening the muscles in your forearm and upper arm. Cease all body movements. Then relax your muscles and allow the cast to fall behind you.

Photo series 35- top: start with rod tip low; mid: lift with forearm and hand; bottom:- stop with forearm in line with shoulder

Most advanced casters use too much speed when they cast for distance. They use their speed and strength to move the rod quickly through the stroke hoping this will give them a greater load. This causes several problems. It is more difficult to stop precisely when you are moving fast. Also, it is more difficult to be smooth with your acceleration if you are focusing on speed. You lose the feeling of the rod bending if you use strength and speed. The beauty in fly casting comes from responding to the feeling of the rod and line interacting as you make the cast. You want to develop a feeling of the rod bending and starting to load. Only then, can you adjust your rate of acceleration and speed, to feel you are bending the rod more deeply as you continue the acceleration. You want to feel the rod bend, and then pull deeper in to that bend. In order to feel the rod, you need to slow down.

Begin by making the back cast with your typical speed and strength. On the next back cast, slow down the acceleration and use half the effort. The cast will still lay out nicely behind you. Make a second back cast, using half as much strength and speed. Again, the cast will again lay out nicely. Make a third back cast, now use just barely enough speed and strength to lift the line. Stop and turn around to look at your cast on the grass. Most likely, it has laid out nicely. As you use less speed, you also decrease the amount of strength used. The entire casting stroke is made with less effort.

Using this exercise, you can begin to realize just how little strength and speed it can take to make a good cast. The value is that, now you can develop a range of rates of acceleration. The acceleration will not be based on your muscle memory and habit. The acceleration will be based on what the rod wants and needs in a given situation. When you develop a range of acceleration speeds, you have options to match a specific situation. If it is a dead calm day, and you are sight casting, you can move your line quietly off the water, and deliver your fly with stealth. Then, on the blustery, rough surf outings, you have extra speed and strength to apply to your cast. This is why you adjust and what helps you become a more adaptable angler.

Back Cast Unloading

Proper loading the rod is only part of the process for a successful, efficient cast. After you create the energy in the rod, you must transfer as much energy as possible into the fly line. The energy in the fly line and the loop is what ultimately gets your cast where it needs to be. The transfer of energy from the loaded rod to the fly line occurs with the stop. The more abrupt and complete the stop, the more energy is transferred to the fly line.

Stopping the rod abruptly is not as easy as it appears, particularly with the back cast. There are no other sports where the arm motion stops abruptly. Also, we are not accustomed to a backward throwing motion. There are some style changes that can help you develop this abrupt stop. Casting in the vertical position, the path of your cast is from your waist up toward your forehead. Your forearm stays aligned with your upper arm and shoulder. This position helps you make that hard or positive stop. Your forearm lifts back and up until you hit your bicep muscle, at this point you cannot go any further back. The structure in your arm creates a physical block to help you stop. Joan Wulff refers to using this body structure as a body block.

The body block can do two things for you, achieve a more complete stop and help you stop in the correct position. The best transfer of energy occurs when the stop is complete. This means you do not slow down gradually, or ease into the stop. Rather you move with acceleration right up until the time you stop. By tightening your arm muscles on the stop it helps to stop all body movement, affecting a more abrupt stop of the rod.

Photo 37--arm structure creates body block

The body block can also help you stop in the correct position. Your most efficient cast occurs along a 180° line. The longer the stroke, the more difficult it can be to move in a straight line. Your back cast stop occurs when your rod hand is 90° from your back cast target area. At the end of your distance cast, you are going faster because you have accelerated over a longer distance and created a greater final speed. When you are moving faster, it is more difficult to stop the movement and momentum. A common mistake is moving your hand beyond 90° to the target, and moving in a curved pattern. The structure of your forearm and upper arm make a physical block to be sure you stop along a straight line. Use this body block to maximize the efficiency of your back cast stop. This will help you make even the longest casts with less effort.

Practice your back casts, focusing on your rate of acceleration. Use only the speed and strength that is needed. Use the body block to make an abrupt, effortless stop. Practice this new back cast being sure to hold each back cast stop position until the line falls to the grass behind you. While waiting for the line to fall, notice how much time it takes until the line falls. This helps with judging your timing for the forward cast. Hold your back cast stop position and evaluate your rod arm position. Look to see if your elbow lifted on the back cast (vertical position). Your hand should be relaxed and there should be a 30-

Photo 38- body block in off vertical

45° angle from the rod butt to the underside of your forearm. Notice the structure of your forearm and upper arm creating your body block. Notice the imaginary line from your thumbnail to your back cast target.

To make a series of back casts, start by making a back cast and letting it fall behind you. Hold your back cast stop position until your line settles on the ground. Point your rod tip on the ground behind you. Turn around in place to face your just landed back cast. With your rod tip still low to the grass, walk backward to remove any slack line. Now you are in position to make another back cast. Continue to use this repositioning to make a series of back casts. Focus on the efficient loading and unloading of the rod. When you feel comfortable with your ability to slow down your cast and make good, abrupt stops, you can move to the back cast in the off vertical position.

Photo 39-hold position and evaluate

Off Vertical Stance: hip and body rotation

Most distance casters and saltwater fisherman cast in the off vertical plane using an open stance. This allows stability with increased body movement and allows for the longer casting stroke used with distance casting. The off vertical plane is a casting plane at an angle away from the casters body, but on the dominant hand side. Allow your forearm and hand to tilt out, away from your body. Your elbow tips in toward your side. You can cast at any angle or plane, which feels comfortable. The maximum off vertical plane is at the horizontal position. In this position, you need higher line speed because the line has less altitude to absorb the effects of gravity. Begin with a casting plane of 45° tilt from your body. Keep your elbow relatively close to your side, so you can use your body structure to help stop the rod. In addition, it is easier to move in a straight line and control your rod's path with your arm closer to your body.

Photo 40-off vertical, elbow close to side

113

A body rotation which Joan Wulff calls a body snap can help you move into this off vertical plane. The body rotation is a quick rotation of your hips and shoulders during the casting stroke. This body movement allows your rod arm to move a longer distance for increased stroke length in the off vertical position. Your shoulders and hips move from facing the target, and turn sideways to the target. The speed of the hip rotation can also contribute to the acceleration of the cast. This improves efficiency while smoothly building the casting stroke speed.

Start in the open stance and looking forward at your target. Your shoulders and hips face forward, but at a 45° angle to your target. Start the cast by rotating your hand and forearm while lifting the line for the cast. Your palm and forearm rotate skyward and your elbow tilts in toward your side. In the vertical plane, when your thumb is on top of the rod butt you can see your thumbnail. In the off vertical plane, your thumb is still on top of the rod butt, yet the entire forearm, hand and rod butt are rotated. Now you see your fingernails and side of your thumb.

Rotate your hand and forearm to the angle you select for your casting plane. As you accelerate your rod arm during the casting stroke, allow your hips to rotate so your rod hand can move on a trajectory up and back toward your body. Your hips rotate to move out of the way of your hand and rod arm. The shoulders also rotate, but concentrate of the hip rotation and allow the shoulders to follow the lead of the hips. Your hips stop when you are turned 90° to the target. Your shoulders will also be 90° to the target. You will be able to look at your palm and knuckles, and your elbow is close to your side. Your rod hand stops in front or even with your shoulders. The end of the body rotation coincides with the abrupt stop. When the hips have rotated and the rod has moved through the casting stroke everything stops. The body block of your upper arm structure can be used with the body rotation.

Photo series 36- L-start position; R- stop position after body rotation

Allow the line to fall to the ground as you did in the vertical position. Turn your head to watch the cast unroll. Be sure not to over rotate your hips and shoulders. Turn just your head and neck to watch the cast. When you have ended your body rotation and back cast stop, move your eyes quickly to the rod tip. By watching the rod tip just after the stop, you can see the loop form and then unroll. This is how you can see the effect of your abrupt stop.

Make a series of only back casts in this off vertical position using the hip rotation and body block. Let each cast fall to the ground. At the end of each back cast stop, hold your position and allow your cast to fall to the ground. While waiting for your cast to unroll and fall, notice your body position. Your hips and shoulders are positioned relatively sideways between your back and forward cast targets. Your hand should now be relaxed, and you can see you fingernails and palm. Check the position of your rod butt relative to your forearm. There should be a 30-45° angle. Notice how much time it takes for the longer cast to unroll and fall to the ground. Practice your back cast in this position making a series of only back casts as outlined above. This exercise is where you will make the majority of gains in your back cast. Most people will spend a considerable amount of time fine-tuning the back cast before moving to the forward cast.

Forward Cast Loading

Loading the rod efficiently for the forward cast involves the same factors as for the back cast. You need to avoid slack line, begin loading as soon as you move the rod tip, start the cast slowly and build speed gradually, and have a smooth acceleration to an abrupt stop. All of this occurs along a straight line to your target. Again, you will need to isolate the forward cast focusing on refinements to this cast. Casting forward comes more naturally to most people. Our muscles are more accustomed to moving in the forward direction, which is required for many sports. This lifelong muscle memory of moving forward with speed, strength and power can cause trouble for the fly caster. These are not the habits, which work best for the fly caster.

Most fly casters use too much speed when they cast for distance. They try to use speed and power to force the rod into a deeper bend, but this does not work. Just as with the back cast, excess speed, power or strength generally detracts from the cast. The longer cast requires a deeper load, but forcing the rod into a bend with speed and power, does not build the load smoothly and gradually. It is fraught with trouble. The crucial part of loading the rod efficiently on the forward cast is to load the rod as soon as you start to move the rod tip forward. You want no wasted effort, and to smoothly build your acceleration. These are the two critical parts of proper rod loading. Your goal is to develop a feeling of the rod bending throughout the casting stroke. You want to feel the rod start to bend then pull more deeply into that bend. This is a subtle feeling that develops over time and can only be developed if you try to work with the rod, not force your strength onto the rod. To build speed gradually and develop this feeling of the rod

Photo 41-- forward cast start position

115

bending, you will need to move more slowly through the casting stroke. As you slow down the cast, you will begin to feel the rod load.

Start by making a back cast in the off vertical position and allowing it fall to the ground. Keep the rod tip up when the cast falls. Then walk forward to remove any slack line. Be sure the rod butt is at a 45° angle to your forearm and your hand has no tension. This is your position for starting the forward cast in the off vertical plane.

Before starting your forward cast, you must determine the straight line trajectory for the cast. When making your longest cast, you will want the cast to unroll well above the target. When the loop has fully unrolled, the line leader and fly will fall to the water as a unit. For distance, the forward cast trajectory is a generally at a shallow angle aimed above the target. For your longest cast, the trajectory will be at or above the horizon. This gives the loop enough altitude to unroll before gravity causes it to fall.

You will be more accurate if you first look at your target before moving your rod arm in a direction. Draw an imaginary straight line from your rod hand to the target. Be sure to aim a few feet above the target. With the forward cast trajectory determined, start moving your rod hand on a straight line toward the target.

Begin the cast slowly using just enough acceleration to move the line. Get the fly line under tension and continue to accelerate, moving your rod hand toward the target. Start the cast by leading with your elbow and finishing with your hand. Do not try to push the rod forward with your hand. Start with no tension in your hand, and think about sliding or sweeping the rod forward. Use body movement in the forward direction to help gradually build speed. Your elbow moves forward first, then your forearm and lastly your hand and wrist. Move slowly so you can

Photo 42-- look forward to determine straight line path to target area

focus on the feeling of the cast. You want to develop a feeling of the rod bending under the weight of the fly line. In the off vertical position, you can watch your hand as you make the cast. Look for your rod hand to travel forward from even with your shoulder to be level or in front of your face. This will ensure that you have moved the rod to get the system under tension and create the loading of the rod. Once the rod is loaded and aligned with the target, you can focus on the unloading or stop.

Forward Cast Unloading

To get an efficient transfer of energy from the rod to your fly line you need an abrupt stop. On the forward cast, you can use the structure of your hand and wrist. You will use the muscles of your hand and fingers with a rotation of your wrist to help stop the rod. Using your thumb pad as an aiming device, move your rod hand along the straight line trajectory for your cast until your thumb pad is directly opposite your target area. When your thumb pad is opposite the target, squeeze your hand. Push forward on the rod butt with your thumb, while also pulling back with your lower fingers. This hand motion creates a quick rotation of the rod butt from the 45° angle to a 0° angle. The rod butt rotates and is now parallel with the underside of your forearm. Your rod is stopped, the cast is complete and your loop begins. Hold this position for a moment while the loop forms, and then relax your hand, having no more tension in your hand.

Watch your forward cast loop unroll. Pay attention to the bottom leg of the loop. This is the line, which is coming off your rod tip. It has already unrolled. Watch for the loop to unroll completely. Lower your rod tip down at the same speed as the line falls from gravity. If you lower the rod tip immediately after the stop, you will rip the loop open and steal power from the cast. If you keep the rod tip up too long, and the loop unrolls and falls. You will have slack line when you lower the rod tip. Develop the habit of watching our loop unroll to gauge how quickly to lower your rod tip.

When casting in an off vertical plane, you need to be sure you stay in the same plane throughout the stroke. Your rod hand and arm should be at the same angle during the entire stroke and on the stop. Only after the stop can you rotate your forearm and hand to the vertical position. If you rotate your hand at any other time, it will create a curve in your loop and steal power from your cast. Be sure

Photo series 37- top: structure of hand and forearm help stop the rod; bottom: rod butt rotates to parallel with forearm

to maintain the casting plane during both the casting stroke and the stop. You can watch your hand and forearm to be sure it does not rotate during the cast.

When the cast has unrolled and fallen to the grass, lower your rod tip and turn around in place so you are now facing the opposite direction. Raise your rod tip up to the off vertical casting plane. Walk forward to remove any slack. You are now ready to make your next forward cast.

Use this turning around in place and walking forward to take out slack, to make a series of only forward casts. When practicing forward casts be sure to make the cast, including the stop in the same

Photo 43-rod remains at off vertical angle on delivery

casting plane. Start each forward cast with no hand tension and a 45° angle of the rod butt to your forearm. Shift your body weight forward. Lead with your elbow, adding your forearm and ending the stroke with your hand. Use the structure of your hand and wrist to close the rod butt angle and stop the rod. Critically watch your loop. Watch the direction, height and shape of your loop. The loop will show if you have moved in a straight line trajectory, stopped on this line, and executed an abrupt stop. If you have executed this properly, you will see a narrow shaped loop aimed at your target area. Remember to follow through by lowering the rod tip at the same speed as gravity affects the lower leg of the loop. Only by critical evaluation can you improve.

Next move to false casting while still focusing on proper loading and unloading the fly rod. When you false cast you are adding the dimension of timing to your proper loading of the rod both back casts and forward cast. You will need to perfect your timing so the line just straightens and does not fall before you start the next cast. As you look to improve your timing, watch the loop unroll. Look for the line leader connection. Notice it is the final piece to unroll. To improve timing watch the loop unroll and when the loop has just a few feet before the line leader connection, you should slowly begin your next cast. You are looking for the unrolling loop to resemble the hook in the letter J. When just a few feet of line remain to unroll, you anticipate the line and leader being straight and slowly start your next cast.

With time, you will want to develop the feeling of the loop unrolling off the rod tip. As you start to develop your timing, you will need to anticipate the line's full extension. The greatest distance casters have perfected their timing and wait for the line to straighten. This fully straight line under tension lasts for just a moment. Once straight, the line will soon fall from gravity. This split second timing is one aspect that distinguishes the expert distance caster. Practice your timing by making a single back cast and forward cast. When you can execute this well, perform a series false casts and work on your timing with continuous false casting.

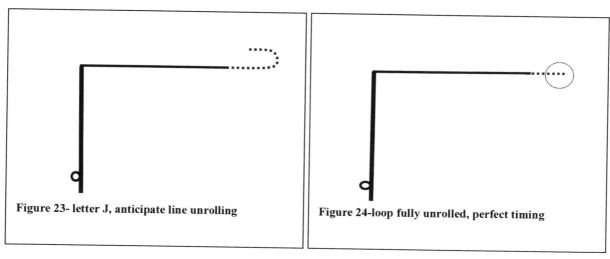

Figure 23- letter J, anticipate line unrolling   **Figure 24-loop fully unrolled, perfect timing**

Load and Unload the rod:
Back cast:
- Start with rod tip load
- Lift with entire forearm
- Build speed gradually
- Use body rotation and body block

Forward cast:
- Determine straight line for cast
- Begin forward cast slowly
- Lead with elbow, finish with hand
- Stop is on the straight line, same casting plane
- Use wrist rotation to stop

Tight Loops

Now that you can more efficiently load and unload the rod, you need to work on forming a tight loop. A tight loop is a loop that is less than two feet wide, meaning from the top leg of the loop to the bottom leg of the loop, there is a distance of less than two feet. Tight loops concentrate the loop's energy in a narrower direction. The narrow loop will have higher line speed and be capable of shooting more line over a longer distance. A wide loop disperses the line's energy over a large area, is less efficient, so less line can be shot. A wide loop also presents more surface area at the front of the loop, which makes it less wind resistant. To understand the effect of a narrow loop containing more energy, think of the nozzle on a garden hose with a set volume of water. If the nozzle is adjusted for a wide spray, the water is dispersed over a wide area with a gentle spray. With the nozzle adjusted for a narrow spray, the water is delivered over a smaller area with greater force. To cast distance, we want the forceful energy of the narrow stream. The tight loop will focus the casts' energy in a narrow direction toward the target. While casting, watch your loop, both the top and bottom legs, and the front of your loop, the nose. The nose of the loop should be narrow, almost pointed. Loops with this shape are aerodynamic. They cut into the wind better, allowing the fly line to maintain energy, which can help you shoot more line for greater distance.

Tight loops are formed by casting on a straight line path. The more precisely you can move the rod along a straight line path, the tighter the loop and the more efficient your cast. You need to move the rod in a straight line away from, and toward your target area. To maintain the straight line path of your rod you also must adjust your casting arc. The casting arc is the angle of the rod from the beginning of the cast to the end of the cast. The rod changes its angle from the start of the cast to the end

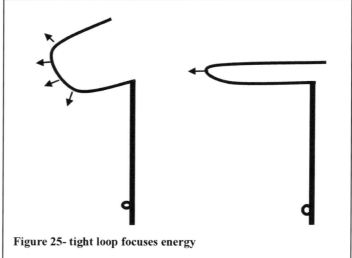

Figure 25- tight loop focuses energy

of the cast (both backward and forward casts), this angle is the casting arc. The casting arc must widen, as the rod is more deeply loaded. If the casting arc is too narrow for bend in the rod, you will get a tailing loop. While the cast is unrolling behind you, relax your wrist slightly to get a wider casting arc and accommodate the deeper bend in the rod. If the casting arc is too wide, you will get a wide loop. The correct casting arc allows the rod to move along a straight line throughout the casting stroke including during the stop. As you cast longer lines be sure to adjust your casting arc and stroke length to achieve tight loops.

To focus on the straight line trajectory and loop formation, isolate each cast beginning with your tight looped back cast. In addition to planning the trajectory, be aware of your stop position. Where you stop the rod, is where you are directing your back cast. Using a clock face for reference, your stop point on the back cast should generally not be beyond the one o'clock position. This is true even in the off vertical plane. If you stop the rod beyond the one o'clock position, you will likely come off the straight line path and move in a curved pattern, resulting in a wide loop. After you stop the rod on the back cast, look at your thumb. The line coming off the thumbnail will indicate if you are moving in a line toward the horizon behind you, or downward toward the ground. Look at the angle between your rod butt and underside of your forearm. This should be not greater than a 45° angle. A greater angle will generally aim your cast downward behind you. If you have a very narrow rod butt angle, you will not get full benefit of the wrist rotation on the forward cast. Keep that angle between 30-45° and you can maximize the wrist movement for the cast.

Photo 44-use thumb to aim cast

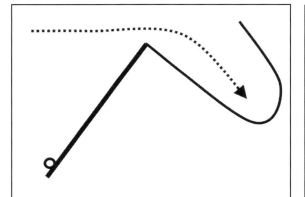

Figure 26- rod tip aimed down on back cast

Photo 45-- use thumb to aim back cast

A useful exercise is to practice aiming your back cast at different targets behind you. Select targets of different heights. Adjust the casting angle so you can aim to unroll your back cast loop over each of the target heights. You may choose a stadium seat for low height, the top of a four foot fence for a medium height, and the top of a small tree for a high target. By practicing with specific targets, you can practice different casting planes, still maintaining a straight line path of the rod.

Photo 46-aim back cast at a specific target

Notice the stop position of your back cast is consistently not beyond the one o'clock position. The imaginary line coming off your thumbnail is pointed at the target, not below the target.

To form a tight loop on your forward cast begin by aiming your cast. Plan a trajectory with the proper casting arc to ensure the straight line path of your rod. When you are casting in the off vertical plane, your rod hand must maintain a straight line toward your target. If you cast at a 45° off vertical angle to start your forward cast, you must finish your cast at this same 45° angle. If not you, will create a curve and have a wider loop.

Remember that your stop must be included on the straight line path of your cast. If you move the rod on a straight line and then rotate your wrist downward on the stop, you will create a wide loop. The straight line cast must include the wrist rotation of the stop occurring along that straight line. This is critical! The stop is part of the straight line.

The wrist rotation on the forward cast contains a slight forward projection within the rotation. It is, not a wrist rotation "in place" or downward. The wrist rotation occurs along the straight line toward the target. It feels more like a projection outward rather than downward. The wrist rotation is more out than down! The wrist rotation occurs while you are moving forward on the straight line and ends on the straight line. The rotation begins when your

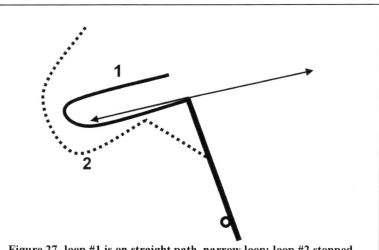

Figure 27- loop #1 is on straight path, narrow loop; loop #2 stopped below straight line path, wide loop

thumb pad is lined up directly opposite the target and occurs while you are still moving forward. The wrist rotation ends when your rod butt has returned to being parallel with the underside of your forearm. There is a 0° angle at your wrist. When the stop is completed, all body motion should stop. After you stop the rod on the forward cast, note the position of your rod shaft. Using a clock face for reference, your stop position will be approximately at the 11 o'clock position. This trajectory will aim your cast high enough to allow the longer line to unroll before gravity takes effect.

After you stop the rod, watch your loop unroll. Watch the bottom leg of your loop unroll, gravity will affect this leg of the loop first. Lower your rod tip at the same rate as this leg of loop falls to the water. This keeps you in contact with the line, and avoids slack. If you keep the rod tip elevated and the leg of loop falls, then you will have slack when you finally lower the rod tip. If you lower the rod tip too quickly, you pull the loop open and steal energy from the cast. Watch for the unrolling fly line and adjust your rod tip lowering by this visual cue.

Tight Loops:
- Cast along a straight line path both back and forward
- Adjust casting arc for amount of rod bend
- Include the stop positions along the straight line path
- Use thumb to aim cast
- Use imaginary line off thumb pad for back cast and thumbnail on forward cast aiming
- Back cast aim at or above horizon
- Forward cast wrist rotation more forward than down
- After forward cast, lower rod tip at speed which unrolling loop falls

Lengthen the Casting Stroke through Drift

Casting longer lengths of line requires a longer casting stroke. It takes more distance to move a longer length of fly line while keeping the line under tension and smoothly accelerating for a greater rod load. If you cast a long line with a short stroke, the line never gets fully under tension before you apply power. You cannot feel the rod loading sufficiently.

The tendency is to compensate for the lack of feeling by applying a burst of power. This generally yields a tailing loop. To properly load the rod and smoothly build speed, you need a longer casting stroke. You have learned to use body movement to give you some increased stroke length (see lesson two). Now you need to add drift to lengthen your stroke even more.

Drift is a repositioning of the rod tip backward, after the stop. This repositioning moves the rod further back, which gives you more stroke length on your next forward cast. Drift is done without power. It is a relaxing back of the rod tip after the stop. The drift move follows the straight line of your cast. It is an extension of the back cast trajectory. The relaxing will be back and up, following the unrolling loop. During drift, your elbow leaves your side as your arm repositions the rod further back. In order to maintain the straight line trajectory watch your loop as you drift. Relax backward in a direction that maintains your loop shape. This will ensure you are drifting at the correct

Photo series 38-top: stop first; bottom: elbow leaves side, rod further back with drift

angle for the cast. You can also watch your back cast target and be sure your rod hand continues to more toward that target during the drift move. After some practice, the direction of the drift, move will feel more natural.

When learning to drift, be sure to make the stop first, and then drift. Be careful not to run the stop and drift together, this is a common mistake. Drift occurs after the stop, when the rod has unloaded. Remember that the stop forms the loop. The loop must form before you can drift back towards it.

Begin adding drift by, keeping the moves short drifting only an inch or two. Focus on the direction of the drift movement. The length of the drift should be matched to the length of line being cast. Ultimately, you will want to develop a range of drifts: short, medium and long, to match the length of the cast. To ensure control over your cast and maintain the straight line, you can use your body structure as a reference to define a maximum drift position. This position occurs when there is a right angle between the underside of your upper arm and the side of your body, and another right angle between your forearm and upper arm. This is the position for your maximum drift as you

Photo 47- use body structure to find maximum drift position

are learning. Using your body structure helps you maintain the straight line path of the cast while you add drift. Ultimately, you may exceed these parameters for your longest 100-foot plus cast. You may find you can increase the forearm to upper arm angle to over 100 degrees. Your longest drift position will be determined by your body structure and your ability to maintain the straight line path of the rod. Once you exceed these parameters, you are more likely to move off the straight line path and ruin your cast.

Drift:
- Occurs after the stop
- Repositions the rod tip further back
- Allows for longer forward cast
- Maximum drift positions: 90°angle of upper arm to forearm and upper arm to body
- Forward cast starts with elbow returning to side

From the extended back drift position, start the forward cast by shifting your body weight forward and moving your elbow back in toward your side. Think of returning to your initial back cast stop position. The forward casting stroke mechanics are the same: body, elbow, forearm, and finishing with the hand. The longer casting stroke allows you to build higher line speed by accelerating over a longer distance. It takes slightly more time to move this longer distance. Focus on slowing down and smoothly building speed. When your elbow has returned to your side, and your hand and forearm are in front of your shoulder, the hips rotate from open stance to forward helping you smoothly accelerate to your target. Make your forward cast stop on the straight line and watch your cast unroll toward the horizon.

Using drift allows you to make longer casts more easily, with a longer, yet smooth casting stroke. It is also keeps you in contact with your line as it unrolls off the rod tip. It gives you a sense of constant tension with the line and adds to your enjoyment of casting. As you practice drift, practice short, medium and long drifts so you can explore the range of drift and find your maximum drift length. After each back cast and drift, stop and allow the line to fall. After the loop unrolls, and has fallen to the ground notice your body position. Look for the maximum drift angles of your body structure. Check to be sure the imaginary straight line from your thumbnail is aimed at your target, not pointed downward.

Photo series 39- top: elbow leaves side on drift; mid: elbow returns to side on loading move; bottom: aim at horizon

False Casting Longer Lines

When false casting longer lines use drift on the back cast and follow through on your forward cast. Follow through on your forward cast gives you more space for a longer back cast stroke. After you stop the rod on the forward cast, allow your rod hand to continue forward a few inches. Like drift, the forward follow through is done without power and occurs after the stop. Your hand is relaxed, and the wrist is in the bent down position. Your elbow moves slightly forward, in front of your body, to allow your hand to move in a direction that maintains the shape of the loop. Now you have lengthened your casting stroke in both directions and can false cast with drift on the

Photo 48- elbow moves forward on follow through, lengthens stroke for next back cast

back cast and follow through on the forward cast. As you false cast notice your elbow movement. Your elbow moves away from your body only after the stops. Focus on the direction of your drift and follow through. These movements should be without power and in a direction, which maintains the shape of the loop.

Remember to relax as you false cast. You should have tension in your rod hand and arm only during the stops. The remaining time of the casting stroke, you should be relaxed. Focus on the slower casting stroke tempo for longer casts and the feeling of the rod loading and unloading.

Trajectory for Distance

The trajectory for longer casts changes slightly. When you are casting longer lines, and plan to shoot on your final delivery cast, you will need to aim the delivery cast at or above the horizon in front of you. The back cast is aimed at the horizon behind you. Normally, you anticipate when the back cast will completely unroll and start your forward cast just before this occurs. For longer lines, you want the back cast to unroll completely. Then allow gravity to take effect and the line to fall just below the horizon. This sets you up for a straight line forward cast that is aimed just above the horizon.

As the forward cast unrolls, allow it to fall to below the horizon. Now you can make a back cast with a slightly upward trajectory. Your casting trajectories become two straight lines that resemble a long sideways letter X: ><. Each cast is aimed high and then allowed to fall slightly so the next cast can again be aimed upward. Practice this trajectory change with your false casting including drift and follow through forward.

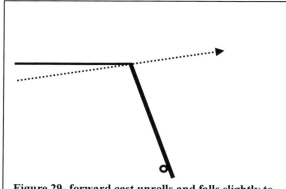

Figure 29- forward cast unrolls and falls slightly to allow upward back cast trajectory

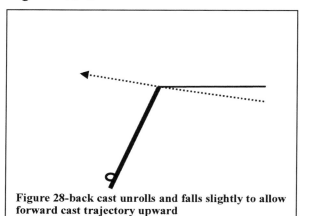

Figure 28-back cast unrolls and falls slightly to allow forward cast trajectory upward

Double Haul

By now, you most likely have learned the double haul. If not, focus on the second lesson, which covers the double haul in detail. In your quest for increased distance, you will need to refine this technique. It has been said that most people use the double haul to cast their mistakes faster and farther. When casting distance many anglers yank on the line with their line hand, pulling as hard and fast as they can. Their haul is not balanced with their rod arm and this is reflected in a poor cast. When hauling, both hands should work together to maximize the bending of the rod. The goal of the double haul is to make your casting more efficient and through this, help you reach your distance potential.

The double haul is a two-direction move. It is a haul and a give back. The haul is a pull on the fly line during the casting stroke and has precise parameters. The haul coincides with the wrist rotation of the stop. Just like the rod hand, the haul accelerates to an abrupt stop. The haul is made in a direction opposite the rod hand. On the back cast, the rod hand moves back and up, while the line hand hauls forward and downward. On the forward cast the rod moves forward and outward and the haul is made down and backward. The haul is only as long as the wrist rotation of the stop. The haul is sharp and the give back is slow. All of these parameters of the haul are matched to the parameters of the cast.

Photo 49-double haul, horizontal position

Photo series 40- top:- line under tension to start cast; mid: line under tension during haul; bottom: line under tension during give back

When refining your double haul begin by focusing on the haul. Is it balanced to the rod arm and what is happening with the casting stroke? The haul should be balanced for speed, acceleration and length. Short casts with a short haul. A long cast with a long haul. Slow casts with a slow haul. Faster casts need a faster haul. Next, be sure your haul is helping the cast and not creating slack. Be sure there is no slack line introduced into the cast. Slack can be monitored by watching the piece of fly line from your first stripping guide to the line hand. This line should always be under tension. It is the line hand's function to be sure this line is constantly under tension. A poorly timed or aggressive haul will create slack. If you cast too fast, it is easy to make a haul that is too long or too fast. The rod hand and haul hand should be matched, not in a race with each other. Balance the rate of acceleration of your haul with the casting stroke. The timing of the haul is important. The haul should not start too soon in the casting stroke. The haul must wait until the rod is loaded and positioned for the stop. Then the haul and wrist rotation occur together.

After the haul watch your giving back of the line. Many casters reach the end of their haul and immediately start to give the line back. Remember that the loop is formed at the end of your stop. This is also when your haul will end. You need to give the loop a moment to develop so when you give the line back, the loop can accept it. If you rush the give back, you will see slack in this piece of line. Slow down the give back and try to feel the energy in the loop gently pulling the line in your line hand. Give back the line only at the rate the loop wants to accept it. This minimizes slack and keeps you in contact with the fly line.

Practice your hauls focusing on the piece of fly line from the first stripping guide to the line hand. Be sure it is always under tension and no slack line occurs. Practice different lengths of hauls: short, medium and long hauls. Develop a range of hauls that are balanced with the length of line being cast. Be sure the line hand returns up toward the reel, so it returns as much line as the loop can accept. This sets you up for your longest hauls, which you will need for false casting longer lengths of line.

To check if your double haul skills are helping you, make a cast with a haul and see how far you can shoot line. Be sure to measure your distance with a tape measure. Next, make a cast with the same effort but without a double haul, and shoot only on your delivery cast. See how far it shoots. Again, measure the distance. The cast with the double haul should cast further than without the haul, or it should allow you to use a shorter stroke length and less effort. This is how you know your double haul skills are working for you.

Double Haul efficiency:
- Hands move in same direction during loading move and separate on the stop
- Haul is:
- coordinated with the stop
- Occurs opposite the direction of the rod
- Accelerates to a stop
- Is balanced to the rod arm movements

- Haul ends when wrist rotation ends
- Give back is slow; at the rate, the unrolling loop can accept it
- Watch line from first stripping guide to monitor for slack

Shoot Line on Back cast

Most people can master the technique of shooting line, but are not necessarily efficient with their shooting line. Many people attempt distance casting by randomly shoot line. They make multiple false casts shooting line with each cast until they shoot so much line that they can no longer control it and the cast falls apart. You should always have a plan when you are shooting line. For distance casting, it is imperative to have a disciplined plan.

The first concept that governs shooting line is to know the head length of your fly line. This is close to the maximum amount of line you will pick up and false cast. Once you pick up the entire head and shoot line, you must understand the concept of overhang. Overhang is the amount of running line outside your rod tip, between your rod tip and the fly line head. It is always easier to control the fly line when the head is close to the rod tip. The further away the head is from the rod tip, the more difficult the line is to control in the cast. With the head far away from the rod tip there is a lot of overhang. Too much overhang creates a hinging effect in your cast. The hinging makes your line more difficult to control from the inefficient energy transfer between the head and the running line. This makes it difficult to maintain a straight line path. You can have some overhang as long as you can control the cast and there is no slack. If you exceed the amount of line you can control by even one foot, you will be out of control and your cast suffers. How much overhang can be tolerated is variable. Every rod and line combination can handle a different amount of fly line and overhang.

An additional distance technique is to shoot line on the final back cast just before the delivery cast. By shooting line on the final back cast, you maximize overhang and carry a maximum length of line only on the forward delivery cast. You are using a technique called preloading. Preloading means that the rod is starting the forward cast with some load. Normally, your back cast unloads and the rod straightens. The rod does not begin to bend again until you start the forward cast. When you shoot line on the final back cast there is momentum from the line shooting backwards as the cast unrolls. When you trap the line to stop the shoot, the act of trapping the line causes the backward line motion to cease. This sudden stopping of the backward motion pulls the rod into a bend. There is a moment that the rod is loaded before you start moving forward, it is preloaded. When you start forward, the rod continues to bend and is loaded even more deeply. This gives you more energy for you forward delivery cast and shooting line. This technique of trapping the line then starting forward requires split second timing. When you capture this moment your cast will have tremendous energy, and you will feel this deeper load in the rod.

Your goal should be to make a distance cast with as few false casts as possible. Only shoot line if you can continue to control the cast. When you reach the maximum overhang you can control, shoot a small amount on the final back cast. Shoot the remaining line on the forward delivery cast. The plan is to make a distance cast with only two false casts. Use the double haul and make a back cast without shooting line. Make a forward cast and shoot some line. Now make a second back cast, shooting a lot of line. Maximize the overhang and get the preloading effect. On the delivery cast, shoot the remainder of your line. That is truly planned shooting line with no wasted effort. Practice shooting line on your final back cast with only the two false casts. Develop your timing for the preloading of the rod. This combination will improve your efficiency and distance.

Shooting Line on the back cast:
- Keep overhang to a minimum
- Shoot line on final back cast for preloading the rod
- Plan shoot: back cast no shoot, forward cast shoot, final back cast shoot a lot, deliver cast and shoot remaining line

Quick Cast

The quick cast is a technique that allows you to cast distance with minimal false casting. The classic use is for bonefishing where you are standing on the deck of a boat sight fishing and waiting to find the fish. Once the fish is located you need to quickly make a long cast, there is no time for excessive false casting. While waiting to cast you need to manage your line to prevent tangles and be ready to make the cast at a moment's notice. The line management involves two aspects: managing the line outside your rod tip that you will cast, and the line at your feet that your plan to shoot.

Start by making a distance cast. This will be the maximum amount of line you intend to shoot. Strip this line back in carefully placing it on the deck of the boat. You want the line to be in loose coils so it will shoot easily. By casting the line out, and then stripping it in, when you make a cast and shoot line, the line being shot comes off the top of the pile. This prevents tangles in your fly line. Keep about twenty feet of fly line outside the rod tip. You will need to manage this line by making loops of line and leader. Start with holding your fly by the bend in the hook. Next, make two or three loops of leader and fly line. Make the loops unequal lengths so they will not tangle. Place the loops between different fingers in your line hand, again so the loops will not tangle.

When you see the fish, or the guide gives you a direction and distance, start the cast by sweeping the rod up for a back cast. Hold on to your fly until the sweeping motion pulls the fly from your hand. Reach up with your line hand to grab control of the fly line. Make a forward cast and haul, shooting a little bit of line. Make a back cast and shoot a lot of line, then make your delivery cast and shoot all the line. Be sure to watch your target throughout the cast so you can place your fly accurately. This is how you can make a cast with only two false casts. It is the minimal false casting, which makes it a "quick" cast, not the speed. Practice this cast by going through the moves slowly which will help you develop your technique.

Summary:

The caster's ability to properly load and unload the rod, the efficiency of their hauls and their physical attributes will determine the maximum distance one can cast. It is easy to spend money searching for the right rod and fly line. New rods and lines are great and may very well help you in your quest for distance. A mismatched outfit or a worn out line, never helps. However, most people have a lot to gain by refining their fundamental casting skills. Couple this with a well matched rod and fly line and you are sure to achieve more distance.

You will never improve if you do not spend time to practice. No great athlete ever reaches his or her full potential without tremendous effort. Even weekend warriors improve only by practicing. The key difference between intermediate and advanced casters is usually quality and quantity of practice time. Use the guide for distance casting in the practice section of this book.

Distance Casting:
- Load and unload the rod efficiently
- Form tight loops
- Add drift for a longer casting stroke
- Efficient shooting line
- Efficient double haul

Advanced Casting Concepts

Accuracy

There are times when you need to be both accurate and cast distance. Casting on the flats to bonefish, tarpon, and permit are the classic examples. Whatever the situation, if you need to cast distance and be accurate, you will want to have the principles of accuracy in your repertoire. Accuracy means placing the fly where you need it to land. The smaller the target area the more crucial accuracy becomes. Accurately aiming your cast has two components. They represent two straight lines: the eye-target line and the hand-target line.

The eye-target line is formed by using your dominant eye to "sight" your cast and determines a straight line from your eye toward your target. The hand-target line is also a straight line. This line runs from your rod hand or thumb pad directly toward the target. These are two imaginary straight lines that you need to visualize when aiming your cast. Joan Wulff calls this an accuracy triangle. It is like the letter V tipped on its side < with the pointy end of the V representing the target area. One leg of the V is your eye-target line. The other leg is the hand-target line.

To be accurate the hand-target line must intersect the eye-target line at the target. The wider the base or separation of the two legs of the V, the more difficult it is to be accurate. As the distance to the target increases and the legs of the V are longer, the more difficult it is to be accurate. The closer these two lines are (the narrower the base of the V), the easier it is to be accurate. To be most accurate you need to align your rod hand and your eye. In the off vertical position, this is easier if you bend at the waist. Now your hand-target and eye-target lines are closer and it will be easier to be accurate.

Photo series 41- top: - hand-target and eye target lines; bottom: - accuracy triangle, imaginary lines meet at target

Accuracy takes planning and practice. Practice with both large and small targets. Practice placing the fly left, right, and in the center of the target, then practice in windy conditions. Use these concepts and the accuracy position: rod hand close to eye. Determine your hand-target line and eye-target line being sure these two lines intersect at your target.

Tracking

The concept of tracking is making sure that your casting loops from back to front are in line with each other. This is one-step beyond just casting in a straight line. You can cast in a straight line on a diagonal that you gives you a slice to the right or left. Tracking is your ability to have the back and forward cast made in a straight line with no lateral deviation. Think of a train track. If you are tracking straight, your cast stays on the track. If you cast with a slice, your cast may be on a straight line, but it is not tracking straight. Your most efficient casts will track in a straight line from front to back. Tracking is frequently a hidden problem when looking for long distance casts or with very precise accuracy.

To evaluate your tracking, set up two ropes on the ground 3-4 feet apart, or use two straight lines on an athletic field Cast in the off vertical plane so your back cast and forward cast both stay within the width of the two straight lines. Watch your loops as you cast. You can see if you are tracking straight and within the lines. If not, adjust your arm movement to keep the back cast and forward cast aligned.

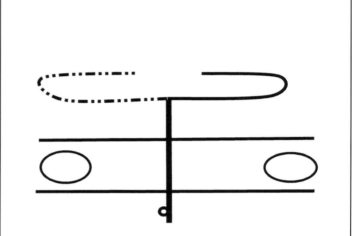

Figure 30- keep back cast and forward cast in-line with each other & target

Tailing Loops

There have been volumes written about the cause and correction of tailing loops. The most important thing to remember is that the rod tip traveling in a concave pattern causes a tailing loop. Somewhere in the stroke, the rod tip dipped down then flexed up, crossing the line and causing a closed or tailing loop. This concave path of the rod tip can be caused many ways. One of the more common ways is by using too short of a casting stroke for the length of line being cast, then hitting the cast at the end. This can be fixed by lengthening the stroke with drift, and increasing the casting arc. You may be uneven with your acceleration to cause the closed loop. This can happen if you focus on speed rather than the acceleration. It is hard to be smooth if you focus on going fast. Alternatively, you may cast beautifully until the final delivery cast. Then, sensing it is the last cast, you hit the cast at the end, trying to give it a little extra power (most common). This results in a burst of power that is not smoothly applied, yielding a tailing loop. You will need to fight your urge to give extra power and focus on being smooth.

Figure 31- tailing loop from concave rod tip path

Part II- Casting Practice

Practicing your casting: How and what to practice

Skill with fly casting rarely comes naturally to anyone. Practice is a crucial element in this skill-based sport. For beginners it can make the difference between success and lifelong enjoyment of the sport, or being overwhelmed, frustrated and giving up. The novice fly fisherman is generally open to the idea of practice, and is motivated by the progress they see with their line control. Anglers can spend a long time being satisfied with their casting skills. As they expand their fishing opportunities or want to perform over a wider spectrum of weather conditions, they find their skills no longer meet their needs. This is when a change is in order.

After fishing for a long time, it can be difficult to make changes in your casting. Your muscles have developed habits. They are programmed with memory to perform a certain way. It takes time and effort to break this old memory and create muscle memory for a new way of casting. Most fly fisherman agree in theory with the need and value of practice, yet they have a difficult time making practice a reality. Many people are stuck because they are not sure what or how to practice. They do not want to practice the wrong things, but are not sure what the right things are. The cast in its entirety is a complex set of actions. In order to change you will need to break the cast down into its components. Focus on each component then begin the rebuilding process. This process of refining your casting skills is not easy.

This section is a guide of how and what to practice. It can save you precious time by focusing your efforts for improving your fundamental skills. Even if you are an accomplished angler, there is usually some aspect you can improve. Much like a professional athlete, one can be gifted and talented, yet never reach their potential without practice. Use this section to guide you in reaching your fly casting potential.

The beginner fly fisherman should focus on the practice exercises that reflect their initial lesson. These include rod arm mechanics, the roll cast, basic cast, false casting and shooting line. This is the core set of skills that all fly fisherman need. These skills allow you to be proficient and begin fishing after a few hours of practice. Which skills to add or refine, and in what order they should be addressed varies for each experienced caster. Your practice needs reflect your prior fishing experience and future goals.

The overview section on how to practice is applicable to all. The "what" to practice, will vary for each individual. First, there are practice exercises that form the basis for all practice sessions. These exercises are the system to use as you practice the content of the casting lessons. Each lesson has a corresponding practice module covering the casting techniques for that lesson. Experienced casters are cautioned not confine yourself to practice only the intermediate or distance casting techniques. I have presented the material in a systematic manner, where the casting skills build on each other to create a solid, efficient and reproducible cast. You should review the material from lesson one. This provides the basis for your detailed analysis in the intermediate and distance casting lessons. The difference in practice from intermediate to advanced caster is in the level of detail to which you hold yourself accountable. Beginning casters should not be overwhelmed by the material and level of detail presented. You should focus on the casting practice for lesson one. Know that in the future when you are ready to advance your skills, you have the information here waiting for you.

Your skill level and ability to perform when fishing is directly tied to your practice. A good practice session can be tough. You must be critical of your cast. If you are not willing to discover your areas of weakness, you will never improve. Remember the purpose of practice is not to focus on what you already do well, but to painfully exam and improve the areas that are difficult for you. You need to get out of your comfort zone and challenge yourself to improve your skills. You cannot be perfect right away. Focus on your ability to improve, and your casting will reflect this.

This section is designed for you to use while you are practicing. Bring the book with you or copy the pages you are focusing on. This will help to guide your practice time and serve as an outline for how and what to practice and evaluate for improvement. Use the information as outlined, or create your own practice sessions. There is unlimited potential. To be successful with your practice time, you need to set up a good practice session. The following helps you to prepare for your practice.

Setting up the practice session

Tackle

Before beginning your practice session, you need to organize your tackle. Be sure your fly line is clean and your leader is in good shape. Remember your leader is the final transfer of energy from your loop to the fly. Be sure your leader is well constructed so it tapers gradually. Do not use too thin of a tippet. You want your leader to unroll fully on the delivery cast. Your casting skills will improve more quickly if you practice tight line casting. This is when your leader unrolls fully to meet your target. It is much easier to add slack for the river presentation casts, than to try to remove slack from your basic casting. I suggest a 9 foot taper leader ending in 8-10 pound tippet (0-3x tippet).

Use a piece of yarn as a fly. This helps you see the end of your leader and where your fly has landed. It is important to determine where your fly lands, not just how much line you cast. Make the yarn fly big enough to easily see, but not so big that it has excess wind resistance.

After cleaning your line, be sure to stretch your line and straighten it. Remove any coils from its being stored on the reel. If the line is in tight coils, it will not shoot well and will not lay out well on delivery. You can stretch the line between your hands until it lays flat. I recommend using a weight forward floating line for most of your practice. If you use sink tips or shooting heads, you should work on the fundamentals skills with a floating line first before adding the weight and momentum involved in casting these heavy lines.

Marking the fly line can help your practice. By marking your line, you know the exact amount of line you are casting. I suggest using a black permanent felt marker and marking your fly line at 40 and 60 feet. Place a single two-inch mark at 40 feet. Place two marks, one inch apart at 60 feet. Use a tape measure to be sure your markings are accurate. Draw the marks around the circumference of the fly line. Allow the marks time to dry before replacing the line on your reel. The marks will likely wear off over time, so you will need to refresh them periodically.

The 40-foot mark will be close to the end of the head of your fly line. This will help you identify the maximum amount of line to pick up for casting. The 60-foot mark helps you judge the length of line you have cast. I know I have cast 60, 70 or 80 feet of fly line depending on whether the 60 ft mark is in my hand, outside the rod tip or a rod length outside the rod tip (assuming a 9 ft rod). This system is simple and allows for accurate judging line lengths from 40-80 ft.

Use targets at all times when casting. This greatly improves your accuracy while developing muscle memory for moving the rod in a straight line toward the target.

Location

The ideal location should be near your work or home so you can easily get to the practice site. Find an unobstructed area that is a minimum of 100-120 ft. long. This will allow for back and forward casts of 50 - 60 ft. If you are focusing on distance, you may need a larger area. Be sure the area is wide enough to cast comfortably and not spend your time in the trees. I recommend using a grass field for initial practice rather than on water. Using a field allows you to isolate the casting moves and focus more on the casting mechanics rather than presenting the line on the water. Save water practice for when you want to practice lifting line off the water, roll casting, or water specific techniques. After you have improved your skills, then you should spend time practicing on the water. The most important concepts are that you do not need water to practice and you need dedicated practice time that is separate from fishing time.

Practice Time

How can you find time to practice? You need to make the time. Like any improvement, such as diet or exercise, fly casting improvement requires a commitment of time. It does not always require a lot of time, but does need some time. You will get the most benefit and see the quickest results in your casting if you spend time practicing on a regular basis.

Install a few hooks in your garage, and leave your practice rod set up and ready to use. This way if you have only 15 minutes, you can still spend time practicing. You avoid the time and excuse of needing to put the rod together. You can just pick up the rod and start practicing in your yard within a minute of thinking about the practice.

Practicing your casting mechanics does not requiring using the entire rod. You can purchase a wooden dowel or use a rod butt for practice. Using the rod butt or dowel, you can concentrate on the movements of the cast. There are practice rods on the market that can be invaluable tools for indoor practice. This is particularly important if you live in an area with a long winter season. You can also use the technique of pantomime, and use just your arm and hand to mimic a cast. This can even be done while you are sitting in your car at a stop light.

As you see improvements in your casting, this will motivate you to continue your practice time. It is imperative that you find some time, ideally every week for practice. Regular practice is how your new skills become part of your muscle memory. Once you have good mechanics, the casting itself is enjoyable and continuous self-improvement becomes a life long journey.

When planning your practice session keep the practice sessions short. The goal of each practice session is to break old habits, develop new skills and build new muscle memory. Several shorter sessions are generally better than a single marathon session. Thirty minutes works well for most people. If all you can spare is 15 minutes, it is still better to practice.

Practice Session

When practicing do not make complete back cast and forward casts repetitively like a machine. In order to gain the most from each practice session you need to break down the casting sequence. Slow down and focus on one aspect at a time. Start each practice session by making several back casts to warm up. After warming up, focus on developing one skill at a time. Move slowly and deliberately through the cast. Do not just cast. Look and think about what you are doing. During your practice session be sure to stop before and after each cast. Before each cast think about what you want to do during the cast. Consider how you want to move or feel the cast. After the cast think about what the cast felt like. Evaluate your body position, and if you achieved your intent. Think about this as you set up for your next practice cast.

Consider the wind. When practicing you want to get the feeling of doing the skill well, so use the wind to your advantage. If you are focusing on letting your back cast straighten, position yourself so your line will unroll with the wind. This will intensify the feeling of the line straightening and help you know when you have it right.

Even if you have more than one area to work on, focus on just one or two skills during a thirty-minute session. You cannot improve everything at once. You need to focus your efforts. As you progress, you can focus on combining these skills in your casting.

End each session with a few complete back and forward casts. Try putting the casting sequence together incorporating the new muscle memory from the skill you have been practicing. Be patient. Do not expect improvement every time. Establishing new muscle memory takes time and practice. Judge yourself not on how the line looks, but on whether you accomplished your new skill in the way you intended. Your skill development will eventually transfer from the practice field to the water and your fishing will improve.

Practice session checklist

- ☐ Plan time each week for practice (fishing time is not practice time)
- ☐ Practice for a short time period: 15-30 minutes
- ☐ Keep your gear ready: line marked, taper leader and small yarn fly
- ☐ Use targets, this helps accuracy
- ☐ Practice on a field without the distraction of water
- ☐ Identify a specific focus for your practice
- ☐ Warm up with back casts
- ☐ While practicing make single casts and evaluate each one. Only after you determine what was right or what needs improvement, make another cast
- ☐ End each session with some complete casts
- ☐ Be happy with small progress and give yourself credit for the time you spend

Your rewards for good casting !

Practice tools and techniques

It is important to keep your practice sessions fun and challenging. This will keep you motivated. This section is designed to help you explore different ways for you to learn and improve your casting.

Many people learn not just by the kinesthetic act of doing, but also through visual and auditory senses. Using multiple modalities to learn can help you learn a skill more quickly. You can use the visual mode by watching yourself cast. Have someone videotape your casting for you to review. Watch the video looking critically at your rod arm mechanics. Next, watch the loop shape. If you do not have access to a video camera, you can also watch yourself by using a mirror or a window to see your reflection as you move through the cast. This technique with a rod butt, dowel or indoor practice rod is a very convenient and effective way to practice your rod arm mechanics while getting instant feedback.

To incorporate the auditory sense, close your eyes to remove visual stimuli. Focus on the sound of your rod as you make the cast. The sound should be high pitched and sweet. If the sound is loud and harsh, you are moving the rod through the air with force. Rather than accelerating through the cast in harmony with the rod, you are being too strong and forcing yourself on the cast.

To change your perspective, sit or kneel on the ground and cast. This is like the casting situation of fishing from a canoe and puts you closer to your target. This helps isolate the movements of your rod arm by minimizing the amount of body movement you can add to the cast.

Casting with your non-dominant hand (left hand for a right handed caster) requires your brain to tell your left hand and arm how to move. It focuses your concentration and acts as reinforcement to your brain and body about how you should move to make the cast. All of these techniques improve your focus, help you break old muscle memory and allows for development of new muscle memory.

Always use targets in your practice. By using targets, you are always working on accuracy and your straight line casting. A cast that looks good but does not land on target will never help you fish. Look around your practice area for objects to use as targets. You may find a tree or a fence post to serve as your target area. Whether you bring your own targets for the ground or select targets at your practice site, having targets for both the back and forward casts is critical. The targets determine the straight line of your cast. To have some fun with accuracy position a Hula Hoop on a pole and try to cast your fly line loop through the hoop. This helps focus on casting accuracy and loop size.

Measure your casting distance do not guess. Use a tape measure being sure to measure the point where your yarn fly lands, not the amount of line you shoot. If your fly and leader land in a mess, your cast did not travel as far as you think. You must measure from the point your fly has landed.

Many of the casting exercises call for using straight lines. You can use an inexpensive rope or two purchased from a hardware store. You can also look for straight lines in your environment. On an athletic field, you can use the white lines that are painted on the field. You can also use the edge of a roof on a house, the top of a fence, or a wire between two telephone poles as a measure for a horizontal straight line.

Experiment with the length of line you are casting. Start with short lengths of line and increase your line gradually. Try casting only 10 feet of line. It takes quite a bit of skill to work this small amount of line and be able to load the rod.

Purposely make a "mistake cast". When you try to make each cast perfect, you do not explore the dimensions of your cast. Purposefully making a bad cast helps you learn the action that created this mistake. By learning how to create the mistake, you can more purposefully avoid doing what caused the mistake. When you are sure of how to make the mistake, you can now be sure of what not to do. You will have more control over the outcome of the cast.

Isolate each cast and focus on just back cast or just forward casts. This allows you focus on a single cast. Making a series of casts in one direction allows you to focus your skill development. When you have improved each cast, you can then put the two casts together. However, start with a single cast focus.

Casting in the vertical position is a technique that allows you to use your body structure to help you move through the casting stroke. This is a great position for accuracy and helps ensure that you cast in a straight line. If you usually cast in the off vertical stance, try the vertical position while you are improving your casting fundamentals.

Using your rod arm only and no line hand focuses on developing the rod arm mechanics. It also eliminates the possibility of the line hand causing problems. You can improve your rod arm mechanics much faster by leaving your line hand in your pocket and using your rod arm only.

Consider a change in your equipment. Use a different rod action or rod weight. Use a softer or lighter weight rod to help you feel the bend in the rod. This helps you realize how excess power and force are hurting your cast. To cast gracefully with a soft rod you will need to back off on the power. Slow down and learn to work with the rod. Using a stiffer rod or a heavier weight rod can help your realize the tremendous power in the spring flex action of the rod. This is accentuated if you first use a lighter rod, then switch to a heavier rod. The stiffer action rod will feel like a sports car. This helps you recognize how little effort you need, and how much the rod and line work for you in the cast.

Fly line design affects your cast. As you progress as a caster, you may begin to notice this factor. As a beginner, you are generally casting shorter lengths of line and a short head fly line works well to load the rod. As you increase your casting distance, changing to a long head fly line can help you. A long head fly line is a line with the head length greater than 40 feet, perhaps as long as 55 feet. Remember that the fly line has weight. The more line you can carry in the air when false casting, the more weight you have in the line to bend the rod. The increased line weight helps load the rod more deeply. This gives you more energy to transfer to the line and a longer shoot. The limiting factor in how much line you can false cast is partly the caster's skill and partly the line design. As you improve your ability to control more line in the air, the longer head fly line allows you to false cast a longer line. The longer head fly line usually has a longer rear taper to help you control the turnover of the loop and avoid the problems of excess overhang. As you progress with your distance casting, it can be fun to use a long head fly line and challenge yourself to perform controlled false casting of longer lengths of line.

If you are working on your roll cast, consider using the Triangle Taper line. This is one of the easiest lines to roll cast. It has a unique taper that has no belly. It has a front taper followed by the head, which continuously increases in diameter until the rear taper then the running line. This means that you have thicker line turning over thinner line (until you reach the running line portion) which translates into easier roll casting. With the entire head length at the rod tip, this line also is an excellent choice for developing your shooting line ability.

For long roll casting a double taper line is great. This line has a front and rear taper, but is the same diameter for the remainder of the fly line. This gives the line a belly of about 80 feet. A roll cast of more than 50 feet would be easiest with this line.

Another type of line that is interesting is the new fly line called Sharkskin. The Sharkskin line has a hard coating that has microscopic bumps. The bumps keep the line floating and prevent resistance as the line shoots through the guides of the rod. The fun part is that these bumps create a noise as the line moves through the guides. This noise provides an auditory clue to your casting. You can hear if the line slips through the guides when you should be maintaining tension on the line. You can hear the line as it is shooting. You can estimate the length of shooting time and how much line was released. You can also listen to the line as you double or single haul. You can hear the haul, the pause (no sound) and the give back. You can listen for symmetry of your double haul from back cast to the forward cast. The sound duration should be similar with the hauls on the back and forward cast. If not, then the hauls are uneven.

Remember to keep your casting practice interesting and fun, using a variety of these tools and techniques will help. It is impossible to determine how much time you will need to invest to improve. One thing is certain: you will never improve if you do not practice. If you create your practice session so it is interesting and fun and you practice regularly, you will see long lasting skill improvement.

Practice tools and techniques

- ☐ Use multiple senses to learn: visual, auditory & kinesthetic
- ☐ Use targets
- ☐ Measure your casting distance
- ☐ Use visual straight lines
- ☐ Vary the length of line you cast
- ☐ Make a "mistake cast"
- ☐ Isolate the back and forward casts
- ☐ Use the vertical position
- ☐ Use the rod arm only
- ☐ Equipment change: rod or fly line

Practice Exercises: Fundamentals

<u>Exercises: Introductory</u>
- ☐ Rod arm mechanics
- ☐ Rod arm mechanics in off vertical and open stance
- ☐ Hand tension
- ☐ Wrist rotation
- ☐ Indoor practice

Rod Arm Mechanics

Rod arm mechanics refer to how your rod arm and hand move to make the cast. This exercise is useful for all stages of casters. If you are a beginner, the mechanics are important to practice because by moving your rod arm and hand in a very precise way, you can ensure a good cast. For the experienced caster, the rod arm mechanics are your key to changes in style that will improve your control of the fly line and rod.

Rod arm mechanics

Arm part	Joint	Action
Hand	Wrist	Holds the rod and stops the rod with tension Wrist: bent down (0°) or straight (45°)
Forearm	Elbow	Moves back and forth to give stroke length
Upper arm	Shoulder	Lifts and lowers to facilitate trajectory and aiming the cast

Key concepts:
- Use all three parts of your arm: the forearm for stroke length, the upper arm for trajectory and the hand for stopping the rod
- Arm parts move in sequence, the movements flow one into the other
- Back cast sequence: forearm, upper arm, hand
- Forward cast sequence: upper arm, forearm, hand.
- Back cast starts with the wrist in the bent down position and finishes with the wrist in the straight position (30-45°)
- Forward cast starts with the wrist in the straight position and ends with the wrist in the bent down position. (0°)
- Back cast hand action is a squeezing of the rod butt, stop near your temple, thumb is upright
- Forward cast stop is a pushing forward with the thumb and pulling back with the lower fingers, starts when thumb pad is lined up with target area
- Hand tension only on the stops
- Follow through to the water after the forward cast stop
- Casting stroke is an acceleration to a stop
- Each cast back and forward occurs along a straight line
- There is a pause at the end of each casting stroke to allow the loop to unroll
- Use the vertical stance keeping your rod hand in line with your upper arm and shoulder to facilitate a straight line path of the rod
- Grip: thumb or forefinger on top of rod butt

Before starting, take a deep breath and relax your body. Be sure your hand has no tension. Use a mirror to watch yourself make the cast. Be sure there is no change in the angle of the rod butt to your forearm until the stop. Move in slow motion so you can see your arm movements throughout the casting stroke. Hold your stop position both back and forward to allow time to evaluate your body movements. Practice this several times while facing the mirror. Then turn sideways so your rod arm is closest to the mirror and cast. Observe your body movements from this position.

<u>Rod Arm Mechanics</u>: Using your rod butt and rod hand only, use a mirror to monitor your movements

<u>Back cast</u>:
- ☐ Start position:
  - ○ Elbow at hip level
  - ○ Hand is relaxed
  - ○ Thumb or forefinger on top of grip
  - ○ Wrist in the bent down position, and rod butt is parallel with forearm
- ☐ Making the cast:
  - ○ Forearm and hand lift inward toward your body
  - ○ Forearm moves in line with upper arm
  - ○ Cast is made on a trajectory toward your temple area
  - ○ Hand squeezes tight on the back cast stop and then relaxes
- ☐ End back cast:
  - ○ Hand is at level of your temple
  - ○ Hand is now relaxed
  - ○ Thumb is upright, not pointed down
  - ○ Rod butt is 30-45° from the underside of your forearm
  - ○ Elbow has lifted

<u>Forward cast</u>:
- ☐ Start forward cast:
  - ○ Wrist is in the straight position
  - ○ Rod butt is 30-45° from forearm
  - ○ Hand is relaxed, no tension
  - ○ Select a target and aim your cast
- ☐ Making the cast:
  - ○ Start by lowering your elbow
  - ○ Maintain the angle of the rod butt, there is no change in the wrist position
  - ○ Move your hand on a straight line toward your target
  - ○ Thumb pad lines up directly opposite target (90°)
  - ○ Wrist rotation: thumb pushes forward while lower fingers pull back
  - ○ Hand has tension during the stop for a moment, then relaxes
- ☐ End forward cast:
  - ○ Wrist is in the bent down position
  - ○ Rod butt is parallel with forearm
  - ○ Hand is relaxed
  - ○ Elbow has returned to hip level

Rod Arm Mechanics

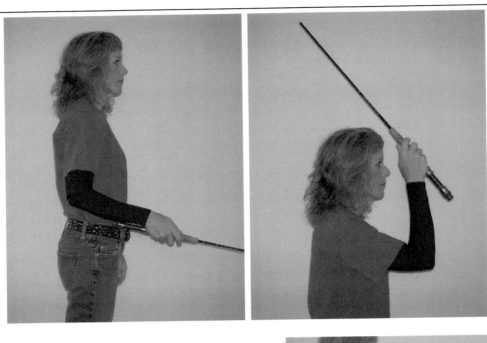

Photo series 42- top: L-R: back cast start and stop positions; bottom: L-R: forward cast stop and follow through positions

Rod Arm Mechanics: Off Vertical & Open Stance

Use the rod arm mechanics exercise to practice the off vertical position. You can add drift when you are ready. In addition to using a mirror or reflective window to observe your rod arm mechanics, look in the reflection for something to help judge your straight line casting. Indoors, you may find the frame of a mirror or the framing on a window to use as a straight edge. Stand side ways to the mirror and use the open stance with a hip rotation for the off vertical position. Make a back cast following the checklist. Add drift when you are ready. Make all the movements slowly so you can watch and feel the sequence of body movements as you cast. Stop and evaluate your body position at the end of each back and forward cast. After making several complete casts (back and forward casts) slowly false cast adding drift on the back cast and follow through on the forward cast.

Key concepts:
- Open stance position: shoulders and hips turn slightly outward
- Hand and forearm rotate up, for the off vertical position as you start to lift the line
- Elbow remains close to your side
- Rod hand and arm stop in front or even with shoulder
- Forward cast starts with elbow moving forward in the off vertical casting plane
- Forward cast continues, with arm sequence: elbow, forearm and hand
- Delivery cast is made in same casting plane, check thumb and wrist for casting plane
- False cast in the open stance

Practice this casting technique using your rod butt only and pantomime the movements. Next, add your rod and a short length of line until you are proficient.

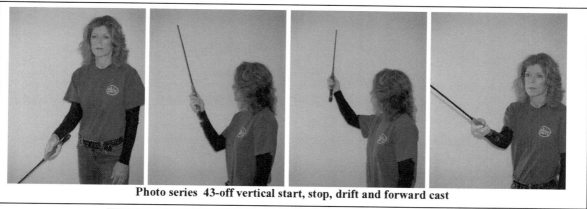
Photo series 43-off vertical start, stop, drift and forward cast

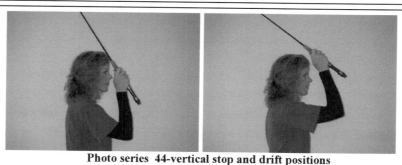
Photo series 44-vertical stop and drift positions

151

Off vertical and open stance mechanics
This exercise can be done with the complete rod (no fly line) or just the rod butt

- ☐ Start back cast:
    - o Use the open stance
    - o Elbow at hip level
    - o Hand is relaxed
    - o Wrist in the bent down position
- ☐ Making the cast:
    - o Forearm and hand rotated outward slightly, placing rod at an angle
    - o Elbow is close to your side, forearm is angled out from your body
    - o Forearm lifts in, toward body
    - o Cast is made on a straight line trajectory toward your back cast target area
    - o Hand squeezes tight on the back cast stop, then relaxes
- ☐ End the cast:
    - o Thumb is upright, not pointed down
    - o Rod butt is 30-45° from the underside of your forearm
    - o Hips and shoulders remain at an angle to the target
    - o Forearm and hand stop in front or even with shoulder
    - o Hand maintains the off vertical angle
    - o Hand is now relaxed
- ☐ Start forward cast:
    - o Hand is relaxed, no tension
    - o Look at your target so you can aim the cast
    - o Wrist is in the straight position, off vertical angle
    - o Rod butt is 30-45° from forearm
- ☐ Making the cast:
    - o Elbow starts the forward acceleration
    - o Maintain the angle of the rod butt, no change in wrist position
    - o Move your hand on a straight line toward the target
    - o Thumb pad lines up directly opposite target
    - o Wrist rotation on the stop: thumb pushes forward while lower fingers pull back
    - o Hand has tension during the stop, holds for a moment and then relaxes
- ☐ End forward cast:
    - o Wrist is in the bent down position
    - o Rod butt is parallel with forearm
    - o Hand is relaxed
    - o Lower rod during follow through
    - o Elbow returns to your hip level

Hand Tension

To practice your hand movements of tension and no tension, use a kitchen sponge. Cut an oval shaped kitchen sponge in half so you have a half moon shape. Wet the sponge and wring out excess water so it is still damp. Hold the sponge in your hand with the curved part under your thumb. Cast with the sponge in your hand, gripping it like it a rod butt.

Key concepts:
- Back cast starts with the wrist in the bent down position and a soft hand
- No hand tension during the back cast stroke
- Tension on the back cast stop
- Relax your hand during the pause when the cast unrolls
- Forward cast starts with no hand tension
- When your thumb pad is opposite the target, push forward with the thumb, pull back with the lower fingers and the sponged is squeezed by hand tension
- Hold tension for a moment, then relax your hand
- No tension during follow through, the sponge should be fully expanded.
- Focus on feeling the sponge being squished on the stops
- Look for the sponge to be expanded at all other times

Hand Tension practice
- ☐ Begin the back cast, no tension, sponge expanded
- ☐ Sponge squeezed on the back cast stop
- ☐ Relax after stop, sponge expanded
- ☐ Begin the forward cast, no tension, sponge expanded
- ☐ Sponge is squeezed on forward cast stop
- ☐ Relax after the stop, sponge expanded
- ☐ Use the sponge with a rod butt and make the cast

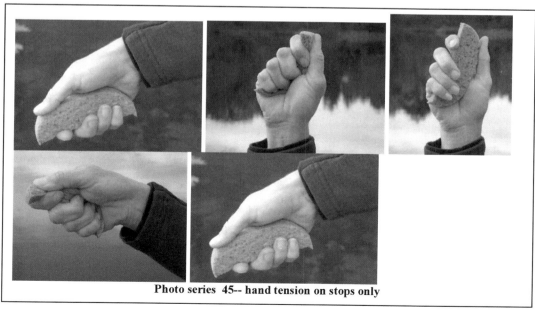

Photo series 45-- hand tension on stops only

Wrist Rotation Practice

The mechanics of the wrist movement are unique to fly casting. Most people need to develop their hand and wrist strength for this movement. This exercise also develops hand-eye coordination using your thumb to aim your cast.

Set up:
- ☐ Use an indoor practice rod or fly rod and 10 feet of line outside rod tip
- ☐ Select a bush or small tree to serve as the target area
- ☐ Imagine a clock face on the target area, with the 12 o'clock position being upright, 3 o'clock is on your right at waist level and 9 o'clock is on your left at waist level

False cast:
- ☐ Begin in the vertical position
- ☐ Select a particular branch to represent 12 o'clock and cast to this specific branch
- ☐ The yarn fly should land lightly on this branch
- ☐ Continue false casting and aiming for a particular branch at other casting angles
- ☐ Make a series of four casts at each target area
- ☐ Increase to a series of eight presentations to each target area when arm strength is increased

Photo 50- develop hand and wrist strength and hand-eye coordination for accuracy

Indoor Practice

Practicing indoors is a valuable part of improving and maintaining your casting skills. You can always find time to practice indoors. For those who live in areas with long, cold winters, indoor practice is crucial to your progress. When practicing your rod arm mechanics, you can use a rod butt or wooden dowel and a mirror (see rod arm mechanics practice). There are a few indoor practice rods available: the Fly-O from Royal Wulff Products and the Echo Mini Indoor Practice Rod. Both are miniature fly rods using yarn or cord to function as the fly line. Typically, one foot of yarn equal 3-4 feet of fly line. In your house, you may want to use just 6-7 feet of yarn, equaling a 24-28 foot cast. Your space will dictate the length of line you can use. Use just your rod arm for this practice.

Key Concepts:
- Regular practice is important to skill development and maintenance
- Allows for brief periods of practice
- Does not require large space
- Use objects in home for targets
- 1 foot of yarn equals 3-4 feet of fly line
- Focus on using your entire arm (all three parts) for the cast
- Focus on moving the rod with acceleration to load the rod
- Hand action to stop and unload the rod, watch loop form

Use the indoor rod to practice the basic cast and to develop your wrist rotation and hand strength for the stop. Use a mirror while casting for immediate feedback. Practice aiming and false casting by standing in front of an object, such as the television. Use the television to resemble a clock face. False cast to all the angles: from 3 o'clock on the right, to 9 o'clock on the left. Remember that from 12 o'clock to 3 o'clock are forehand casts. The 11 to 9 o'clock positions are off shoulder or backhand casts. You will need to change your stance and the fly line will be over your left shoulder. To practice aiming you can cast to a narrow slot between objects in the room. You can also cast under a table to simulate an overhanging branch. Practice changing directions using drift time. Look around your area and find objects and structure that can simulate fishing situations.

<u>Indoor practice</u>
Use indoor rod and practice the following:
- ☐ Rod arm mechanics
- ☐ Basic cast
- ☐ False casting
- ☐ Timing
- ☐ Loop size and shape
- ☐ Accuracy
- ☐ Casting in all planes, backhand and forehand
- ☐ Changing direction
- ☐ Developing hand and wrist muscle of the stop

Photo 51- any object can present a target area

Introductory Casting Techniques: Lesson One

All casts are described for a right-handed caster. Off shoulder casting, refers to casting on the left side of your body. Left handed casters will need to adjust the instructions. When casting with the rod hand only, the line should be secured under the rod hand middle finger to maintain tension on the fly line. Unless specified, casting will be with the rod hand only. The line hand can be in your pocket or to the side, but do not touch the fly line. When an exercise requires two hands, the line hand is added. This is the left hand for a right handed caster.

Use the checklists to help you evaluate each stage of the cast or technique you are learning. Use the details in the lists to evaluate yourself. If you have met all the details, the cast will be good.

Casting techniques:
- ☐ Roll cast
- ☐ Basic cast
- ☐ False casting
- ☐ Shooting line
- ☐ Casting in all planes

Roll Cast

The roll cast can be practiced on a pond or on a grass field. Practice on the water allows you to see your cast unroll toward your target area. You can evaluate loop shape and the cast's energy to see if you can successfully present your fly. It is important to spend some time practicing the roll cast on water. There is value in practicing the roll cast on grass. In this case, you avoid the hassle of getting to the water and the distraction of fish when you should be practicing. To practice roll casting on grass you will need a clipboard or, some way of securing your yarn fly and leader to provide tension when you cast. With the line secured, the loop does not completely unroll so you can see its shape and size easier.

The roll cast allows you to focus on the forward cast only. This decreases the complexity of learning to fly cast. There is no timing between casts. Take your time. Be sure to have a good set up and then make the forward cast.

Key concepts:
- Forward cast only
- Allows learning forward cast in slow motion
- Requires a set up phase followed by the forward cast
- Need "D" shaped loop with line behind the rod tip
- Rod must be tilted out to side to avoid being hit by the fly line
- Stop and allow line to settle before making forward cast
- Perform your check list prior to the forward cast
- Aim with your elbow
- Cast so the fly line does not cross itself (line on the right, cast to the left)
- Wind and line placement determines casting from the right or left shoulder
- Casting stroke starts slowly and builds speed to the stop
- Wrist rotation on the stop
- Watch your loop shape, you want an oval shaped loop that can cut into wind

Photo series 46- top: L-R: roll cast set up: normal and off shoulder, bottom: practice on grass with clip board

Roll cast: Start with 40 ft of line (the 40 ft mark at your reel), and secure the yarn fly under the clipboard if on grass. Be sure to trap the fly line under your middle finger to maintain tension on the line.

- ☐ Set up:
  - ○ Closed stance
  - ○ Lift and tilt the rod way from your body
  - ○ Position your arm to a stop, allow the line to slide back, behind the rod tip
  - ○ Aim the cast by pointing your elbow
  - ○ Check your position:
    - ▪ hand at forehead height
    - ▪ line on the water in front and behind you
    - ▪ D shaped loop behind you
    - ▪ hand relaxed
    - ▪ elbow in line with target area
- ☐ Forward cast:
  - ○ Starts with elbow lowering
  - ○ Wrist is in the straight position (45° angle)
  - ○ Wrist maintains its position, no change in rod butt angle
  - ○ Hand accelerates along a diagonal straight line to the target
  - ○ Wrist rotation begins when thumb pad is lined up opposite the target (90°)
  - ○ Hand tension on the stop: thumb pushes forward and lower fingers pull back, rod butt angle closes
  - ○ Watch loop shape and energy
  - ○ Hand is relaxed after the stop
  - ○ Lower rod tip to the water during follow through (without power)

- ☐ Off shoulder roll cast:
  - ○ Change stance
    - ▪ right foot forward
    - ▪ left foot back
    - ▪ shoulders and hips turned to the left
  - ○ Lift and tilt so line falls over left shoulder
  - ○ Elbow tilts out from body
  - ○ Thumb stays in front of face
  - ○ Aim to target on your right
  - ○ Forward cast as above

Basic Cast

The basic cast adds a back cast to your forward cast. You need to develop your back cast and the timing between the back and forward casts. As a beginner, you will need to develop a feeling of breaking the resistance of the fly line on the surface of the water and learning the correct rate of acceleration to lift the line. You should spend some practice time on water to develop these skills. Later, practice on grass is helpful to allow you to move slowly through the cast and focus on the mechanics.

Key concepts:
- Start with the line straight on the water
- Use the closed stance, facing your target
- Back cast starts with wrist in the bent down position, thumb on top, relaxed hand
- Rod tip is close to the water
- Lift hand and forearm as a unit toward your temple
- Start slowly, building speed gradually
- Watch for the V wake as you lift the line
- Lifting the rod is the loading move and bends the rod
- Stop when you reach the line-leader connection
- Wrist rotation occurs naturally by squeezing your rod hand, creates a slight wrist movement
- Back cast ends with wrist in the straight position, rod butt now 30-45° from forearm and hand relaxed
- Pause to allow loop to unroll behind you
- Start the next forward cast when vibration in rod has stopped
- Forward cast is like the roll cast, but is less forceful because the line is in motion, not static

The water provides a visual cue for the correct speed of the lift. Watch for the wake as you lift the line. You want a little speedboat V shaped wake, not a wide spray. Be sure to relax your hand after the back cast stop so you can feel the rod butt stop vibrating. Now begin your forward cast. If you hear a cracking or whip sound, you have been too quick to start forward. Take a deep breath. Relax while the cast unrolls and then start the forward cast.

If you have difficulty with combining the back and forward casts, you can work on just the back cast. Make the back cast and allow the line fall to the ground behind you. This will not help your timing, but it can help you focus on the lift and back cast stop. You can add timing when you are ready.

Make several basic casts. Watch the water on the back cast pick up. Next, monitor your timing from back to forward cast. Lastly focus on your forward cast. Be sure to include practice on your off shoulder side as this will help you in fishing situations.

Photo series 47-: basic cast: top L-R: start, lift to line-leader connection, bottom L-R: stop and forward cast

Basic Cast
- ☐ Back cast
  - o Roll cast to straighten line on the water
  - o Start with rod tip low to the water
  - o Wrist in the bent down position
  - o Relaxed hand, no tension
  - o Forearm and hand move as a unit to lift the line off the water
  - o Watch the line spray off the water, want a V shaped wake as you lift
  - o Lift until you reach the line-leader connection
  - o Squeeze the rod butt to stop the rod
  - o Wrist is now in the straight position
  - o Thumb is upright
  - o Rod butt is a 30-45° angle to forearm
  - o Relax your hand and hold your position while the line unrolls
- ☐ Forward cast
  - o Starts when loop has unrolled and rod butt vibration has stopped
  - o Look at your target area
  - o Lead with the elbow: cast starts slowly and builds speed gradually
  - o Hand accelerates along a diagonal straight line to the target
  - o Thumb pad lines up directly opposite the target (90°)
  - o Wrist rotation: thumb pushes forward while lower fingers pull back
  - o Hand has tension during the stop for a moment and then relaxes
  - o Rod butt rotates to be parallel with forearm (0° angle)
  - o Lower the rod tip to the water without power, during follow through

- ☐ Off shoulder
  - o Change stance to off shoulder:
    - ▪ Right foot forward
    - ▪ Left foot back
    - ▪ Shoulders and hips slightly rotated to left
  - o Hand and forearm tilt in, toward your body
  - o Elbow tilts out from side
  - o Keep rod hand in front of your face, to maintain straight line trajectory
  - o Aim forward cast with thumb, straight line to target area

False Casting

After you feel proficient with the basic cast, begin false casting. Now you are adding the line hand. You must be sure there is no slack line. Start with 30 feet of line outside the rod tip. Strip off 2-3 feet of line to allow space between your hands when false casting. Watch the line from your first stripping guide to your line hand and be sure there is no slack. This line should always be under tension.

Key concepts:
- Line hand has responsibility to be sure there is no slack line in the cast
- Line hand pinches the line during the cast
- Line hand is positioned slightly lower and apart from the reel
- Line hand moves in unison or parallel with the rod hand
- Line hand lifts and lowers to follow the rod hand movements
- Forward cast is not allowed to touch the water
- Trajectory changes to allow the cast to unroll above the target
- Opportunity to work on timing between casts
- Anticipate the cast unrolling, watch for candy cane hook at end of loop for timing cue
- Hand tension on the stops and relaxed during the casting stroke
- Loop control: watch loop size and adjust casting arc for good loop
- Use all three parts of your arm when false casting: elbow lifts and lowers, forearm moves back and forth, wrist opens and closes
- Arm movements are smaller when false casting, but still present

Photo 52- line hand maintains tension on fly line

While false casting focus on the loops being sure they have an oval shape. Be sure you have good, crisp stops on the back and forward casts. Monitor your timing; listen for the sound of your line as it unrolls. There should be no cracks or whip noises. Use enough speed to give your cast some power, but not too much to cause extra wiggles and squiggles. Be sure the elbow lifts and lowers, and relax while you false cast. Limit false casting to a series of four casts to maintain your concentration.

<u>False cast</u>
- ☐ Strip off two feet of line so you have room for both hands to move
- ☐ Line hand pinches the line between thumb and index finger
- ☐ Make usual back cast
- ☐ Watch the line to be sure there is no slack between your line hand and first stripping guide
- ☐ Aim the forward cast out at the horizon or several feet above the target
- ☐ Do not let your cast hit the water in front
- ☐ Watch your loop size: if they are big you are moving in a wide arc, curved pattern
- ☐ Adjust the casting arc to keep it tight for more narrow loops
- ☐ If you get a tailing loop, most likely the casting arc is too narrow and needs to widen
- ☐ Watch the angle of the rod butt on the stops to monitor the casting arc
- ☐ Monitor rod arm movements: forearm moves back and forth, elbow lifts and lowers, wrist opens and closes
- ☐ Must have a loading move before the stop or you get a tailing loop
- ☐ Watch your loops unroll in front of you and anticipate when the loop is almost unrolled
- ☐ Look for the loop to resemble the hook of a candy cane and anticipate the next cast
- ☐ Listen to your timing between casts, no cracking noises
- ☐ Relax your hand between casts to feel the rod butt stop vibrating for good timing
- ☐ Tension only on the stops, no tension within the casting stroke

Shooting Line

Start with 30-35 feet of line out of the rod tip to false cast. Strip off five feet of additional line for shooting. Begin with shooting line on just the final forward cast.

Key concepts:
- Loop is formed after the stop
- The energy in the loop pulls the extra fly line for the shoot
- The line hand thumb and index finger form a circle for controlled release of line on the shoot
- Tendency is to release line too early, watch for the loop to form after the stop, then release line for the shoot
- Amount of line you can shoot is determined by weight outside the rod tip and fly line design
- Maximum line to false cast is the head length
- Need good crisp stops to unload the rod with energy in the loop
- Aim cast above target to allow time for cast to unroll with extra line from the shoot

When you are comfortable with shooting on the delivery cast, you can shoot a small amount of line on each forward cast by pinching and releasing the line. For a longer shoot, make an extra hard stop on your last back cast. This stronger stop gives more energy to the loop. When you false cast and shoot line, remember not to exceed the head length for the total amount of line you are false casting.

Photo 53-thumb and finger form a circle to control line shoot

Shooting Line
- ☐ Start with casting 30 feet of line and 5 feet for shooting
- ☐ False cast the line
- ☐ Watch the rod tip to see the loop form after the stop
- ☐ Line hand pinches the fly line with thumb and index finger
- ☐ Watch your line hand to be sure there is no slack line during the cast
- ☐ Shoot line on your final forward cast after you see the loop form
- ☐ Change your line hand fingers from pinching the line to a circle
- ☐ Line hand holds the line when the cast is completed and you lower the rod tip
- ☐ After the cast, place the line under your middle finger, preparing to strip line if needed for fishing
- ☐ With practice, shoot line on each forward cast while false casting
- ☐ Re-pinch the line after the shoot, then release on the next forward cast

Casting in All Planes

To handle the obstacles and different conditions when fishing, you need to cast in many different angles. Casting in all planes refers to being able to cast from horizontal on the right, through horizontal on the left.

Key concepts:
- Need to cast at all angles or planes
- Use clock face reference for casting angle: 12 o'clock, 1 o'clock etc.
- Cast on right side of body for 12 o'clock through 3 o'clock, forehand casting
- Right side casting uses the open stance
- Cast on left side of body for 11 o'clock through 9 o'clock, backhand casting
- Left side casting use off shoulder stance
- Right side casting elbow stays close to body, forearm and hand tilt out, palm toward sky
- Left side casting elbow tilts out from body, forearm and hand tilt in, palm toward ground
- Casting mechanics remain the same: load the rod, aim and then stop with wrist rotation
- Obstacles in the environment, wind or location of fish determine which angle to select
- Cast in a straight line, to avoid a slice
- Keep rod hand close to eye to improve accuracy
- Backhand casting: keep hand in front of face to improve accuracy
- Bend at waist to improve hand-eye coordination with 3 o'clock and 9 o'clock position
- Changes in angles are made while the back cast is unrolling: use drift time
- Eyes lead the cast: Always look at the forward cast angle and target before beginning the cast

When casting on a field, use the branches on a small tree or large bush for targets at all angles. Imagine the clock face for reference and practice at all angles. Change the casting angle while the back cast is unrolling. Be sure to look ahead and aim for the next forward cast position. Remember to relax your hand and arm between casts. You can change from forehand to backhand angles while the cast unrolls using drift time. Casting at all angles will help you to change directions and deal with wind conditions. Make a few false casts at each angle before a change.

Forehand casting:	Backhand casting:
Elbow tilts in, towards your side	Elbow tilts out from your side
Forearm and hand rotate outward at an angle	Forearm and hand tilt in toward body, hand is in front of face
Open stance position	Off shoulder position

Photo series 48- top: forehand and off shoulder casting planes; bottom: closed stance

Fly Casting: A Systematic Approach

Casting in all planes:

Forehand casting
- [ ] Begin casting on your right hand side
  - o Use the closed stance, vertical position, casting at 12'oclock position
  - o Make two false casts
- [ ] While the 2nd back cast is unrolling move to the 1 o'clock position
  - o Move your head and look at the 1 o'clock position
  - o Use the open stance: right foot is back, shoulder and hips turn outward slightly
  - o Hand and forearm and tilt out to match the 1 o'clock angle
  - o Elbow tips in toward your side
  - o False cast at the 1 o'clock position
- [ ] Move to the 2 o'clock position
  - o While last back cast is unrolling
  - o Turn and look at the 2 o'clock position
  - o Palm and forearm tilt out a little more, to match the 2 o'clock angle
  - o Elbow remains in toward your body
  - o Right foot is back using the wider based, open stance
  - o False cast in this position
- [ ] Move to the 3 o'clock position
  - o While last back cast is unrolling
  - o Turn and look at the 3 o'clock position
  - o Hand and forearm tilt out flat, horizontal position, with palm and forearm facing to the sky
  - o Bend at the waist to enhance your hand-eye coordination to the target
  - o Right foot remains back using the wider based open stance
  - o Elbow remains in toward your body
  - o False cast in this position

- [ ] Move back to the 2 o'clock position
  - o While last back cast unrolls
  - o Turn and look at the 2 o'clock position
  - o Stand upright
  - o Hand and forearm tilt in to match the 2 o'clock angle
  - o Elbow close to side, moves slightly to allow forearm rotation
  - o False cast in this position
- [ ] Move to the 1'oclock position
  - o While last back cast unrolls
  - o Turn and look at the 1 o'clock position
  - o Hand and forearm tilt in to match the 1 o'clock angle
  - o Elbow close to side, moves slightly to allow forearm rotation
  - o False cast in this position

□ Move back to the 12 o'clock position
- While last back cast unrolls
- Turn and look at the 12 o'clock position
- Move to the closed stance, vertical position
- Hand and forearm move to be aligned with shoulder
- Elbow close to side
- False cast in this position

Backhand- Off shoulder (make at least 2 false casts at each position)

□ Begin casting on your right hand side
- Use closed stance, vertical position, casting at 12'oclock position

□ While the 2nd back cast is unrolling move to the 11 o'clock position
- Move your head and look at the 11 o'clock position
- Use the off shoulder stance: right foot is forward, shoulder and hips turn slightly left
- Hand and forearm and tilt in to match the 11 o'clock angle
- Elbow tips out from your side
- Rod hand remains in front of face

□ Move to the 10 o'clock position
- While last back cast is unrolling
- Turn and look at the 10 o'clock position
- Palm and forearm tilt in a little more, to match the 10 o'clock angle
- Elbow tilts outward a little more away your body
- Left foot is back using the off shoulder stance
- Rod hand remains in front of face

□ Move to the 9 o'clock position
- While last back cast is unrolling
- Turn and look at the 9 o'clock position
- Hand and forearm tilt in, horizontal position, palm and forearm facing down
- Bend at the waist to enhance your hand-eye coordination to the target
- Keep your rod arm flat and look under the rod to maintain hand-eye coordination
- Left foot remains back, using the wide based, off shoulder stance
- Elbow is out from your body, at horizontal position

□ Move to the 10 o'clock position
- While last back cast is unrolling
- Turn and look at the 10 o'clock position
- Stand upright
- Hand and forearm tilt, to match the 10 o'clock angle
- Elbow moves in, toward your body to match the 10 o'clock angle
- Left foot remains back using the off shoulder stance
- Rod hand remains in front of face

☐ Move to the 11 o'clock position
- o While last back cast is unrolling
- o Turn and look at the 11 o'clock position
- o Hand and forearm and tilt to match the 11 o'clock angle
- o Elbow tilts inward, toward your side
- o Off shoulder stance
- o Rod hand remains in front of face

☐ Move back to the 12 o'clock position
- o While last back cast unrolls
- o Turn and look at the 12 o'clock position
- o Move to the closed stance, vertical position
- o Hand and forearm move to be aligned with shoulder
- o Elbow close to side
- o False cast in this position

Practice Exercises: Advanced Casting

Both the intermediate and distance casting techniques use the same practice exercises. First, the exercises are presented so you can understand how to perform the exercise drills and organize your practice session. The details of the casting techniques for the intermediate and distance casting lessons follow. Read the practice exercises first to understand how to practice. Next select a casting technique to improve and use the exercise that helps you focus on that technique. Use these pages as a checklist to guide and evaluate your practice.

Advanced casting exercises:
- ☐ Isolate the cast
- ☐ Horizontal casting
- ☐ Casting form
- ☐ Visual straight line casting
- ☐ Two straight lines
- ☐ Back cast aiming
- ☐ Continuous false casting
- ☐ The one cast

Isolate the Cast

Most people can gain from improving their fundamental casting mechanics. You can never do this by making complete casts. You need to isolate each cast. This is a core technique to being able to improve. By isolating each cast, you can make a series of only back or forward casts and work exclusively on your area of focus for that practice session. Then you can rebuild your cast, fine-tuning your skills and developing new muscle memory to solidify your new skills.

Back cast:
- ☐ Start position
- ☐ Start with the line straight in front of you and no slack line
- ☐ Place your rod tip low to the grass, this allows you to start loading the rod immediately
- ☐ Stand in the closed stance, with your shoulders square to the target
- ☐ Begin with the vertical casting plane: forearm in line with your upper arm, facilitating moving in a straight line
- ☐ Wrist in the bent down position, rod butt is parallel with forearm
- ☐ Hand is relaxed
- ☐ Use the thumb on top grip
- ☐ Trajectory of back cast is back and up, aim the cast to unroll over an imaginary fence behind you
- ☐ Lift the line by using your entire forearm and hand as a unit
- ☐ Lift your forearm up on a diagonal path toward your temple
- ☐ You can see and feel your elbow rise, this ensures an upward as well as backward trajectory
- ☐ Wrist stays in the bent down position during the lifting of the line
- ☐ Use just enough acceleration to lift the line, the rod will bend under this weight
- ☐ The lift ends when you reach the line leader connection (end of the loading phase)
- ☐ Stop the rod by squeezing your rod hand tightly and tightening the muscles in your arm to cease all motion (unloading the rod)
- ☐ Relax your hand
- ☐ Hold your back cast stop position and evaluate your stop position: thumb is upright, rod butt is 30-45°to forearm, forearm is in front of upper arm, elbow has lifted, hand has no tension
- ☐ Allow the cast to fall to the ground behind you
- ☐ Lower the rod tip to the ground behind you
- ☐ Turn around in place to face your just landed back cast
- ☐ Take a few steps backward to remove slack line
- ☐ Make another back cast
- ☐ Off vertical casting plane: use open stance, tilt elbow in and forearm out, turn your head to watch the cast

Use this exercise to focus on:
- Rod arm Mechanics
- Change in wrist positions from the start of the cast to the end of the cast
- Use of the body block for an abrupt stop
- Rate of acceleration of the back cast lift
- Application of power on the stop
- Tight loops and straight line casting
- Developing your back cast hauls, double and single
- Practicing shooting line on your back cast
- Practice aiming your back cast
- Practice back cast at all angles

Photo 54- start position, line straight, rod tip low

Photo series 49- -back cast stop, note wrist & arm position

Forward cast:
- ☐ Start position
- ☐ Start by making a back cast and allowing the line to fall behind you
- ☐ Walk forward a few steps to remove any slack line
- ☐ Stand in the closed stance, with your shoulders square to the target
- ☐ Begin with the vertical casting plane: forearm in line with your upper arm, facilitating moving in a straight line
- ☐ Wrist in the straight position: rod butt is 45 ° to forearm
- ☐ Hand is relaxed
- ☐ Use the thumb on top grip: thumb is upright
- ☐ Trajectory of forward cast is an imaginary diagonal straight line toward the target
- ☐ Start the acceleration by leading with the elbow (feel the elbow lower)
- ☐ Accelerate through the casting stroke sequence: upper arm, forearm, then hand
- ☐ Focus on feeling that you are dragging or pulling the line forward
- ☐ Be sure your wrist stays in the straight position during loading of the rod
- ☐ Use just enough acceleration to move the fly line toward your target, creating a bend in the rod
- ☐ Move your rod hand forward to load the rod until your thumb pad is positioned opposite the target
- ☐ Stop the rod by squeezing your rod hand: push forward with your thumb, while pulling back with the lower fingers for the wrist rotation
- ☐ Relax your hand
- ☐ Hold the forward cast stop position and evaluate your position: wrist is in the bent down position, rod butt is parallel with forearm (0°) and hand is relaxed
- ☐ Watch your loop unroll and allow the cast to fall to the ground
- ☐ Lower the rod tip to the ground
- ☐ Turn around in place to face the opposite direction
- ☐ Raise the rod tip up so you are in the forward cast starting position again
- ☐ Take a few steps forward to remove slack line
- ☐ Make another forward cast
- ☐ Off vertical casting plane: use open stance, tilt elbow in and forearm out, rotate your head to watch the cast

Use this exercise to focus on:
- Rod arm mechanics
- Change in wrist positions from the start of the cast to the end of the cast
- Use of the forward cast wrist rotation for an abrupt stop
- Rate of acceleration of the forward cast
- Application of power on the stop
- Tight loops and straight line casting
- Developing your forward cast hauls, single and double
- Practicing shooting line on your forward cast
- Practice aiming the forward cast
- Practice casting at all angles

Photo series 50- forward cast start and stop positions

Horizontal Casting

One of my favorite practice exercises is casting in the horizontal position. When making a fly cast, it happens quickly. Even a slow tempo cast of 30 feet takes only a few seconds to execute. When a cast is not perfect, it can be difficult to determine what went wrong. This exercise allows you analyze the cast. You can see stroke length, timing, speed and power. These are the elements of the cast, which are variable. They need to be adjusted for each length of line and the fishing conditions. This exercise develops your skill with horizontal casting which is also a very practical fishing cast. If you could have only one exercise to perfect your casting, I would choose the horizontal casting. I do not think you can ever outgrow its usefulness.

Key concepts
- Stroke length: how far your rod hand moves during the casting stroke
  - Too short: the fly lands above your target and is likely to create closed or tailing loops
  - Too long: the fly lands below your target and you get a wide loop
  - Perfect length: fly lands on target

- Timing: between forward and back casts
  - Too quick: the line is going in both directions and you may hear a crack or whipping noise
  - Too slow: the line sags, starts to fall, and you lose tension in the line and rod
  - Perfect timing: maintains tension in the fly line

- Speed: how fast you move during the casting stroke
  - Insufficient speed: the line never gets under tension and your rod does not load or bend
  - Too much speed: too much energy in the line, likely to miss the stop point when moving fast
  - Perfect speed: rod loads gradually (acceleration) and line is under control throughout the cast

- Power: how much strength in your hand on the stop
  - Not enough power: the loop barely forms; there is no abrupt stop, but a gradual slow down and inefficient unloading of the rod
  - Too much power: the line has wiggles or bumps in the line which is slack and the line is not under tension
  - Perfect timing: the line stays under tension with no extra wiggles
- Forearm and hand move horizontal (side to side) during the casting stroke
- Wrist angle opens on the back cast and closes on the forward cast

This exercise is done on a grass field. Start with 30 feet of line, and as you improve, increase to 40 feet. Ultimately, work with the entire fly line head outside the rod tip. Start by allowing each cast to fall then progress to false casting.

Set up:

- ☐ Place the rod on the ground and position the line out of the rod tip at a right angle
- ☐ Extend the line so it is straight
- ☐ Place a target a foot or two beyond the yarn fly
- ☐ Start with a three foot round target, such as a hula hoop, use smaller targets as you progress
- ☐ Walk the fly line to the other side of the rod, creating a right angle from the rod tip
- ☐ Straighten the line and leader
- ☐ Place the second target a foot or two beyond the yarn fly
- ☐ Both targets should be in line with your rod tip

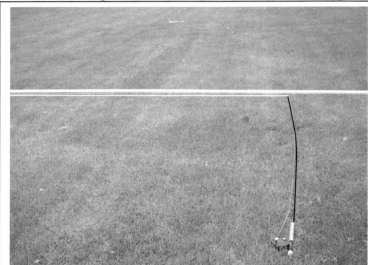 

Photo series 51- -set up two targets in line with rod tip

Horizontal casting exercise:

- ☐ Start by isolating each cast in the horizontal plane
- ☐ Stand with your feet on either side of the rod, toes pointed straight ahead.
- ☐ The targets are on each side, at the level of your rod tip
- ☐ Hold the rod with your usual thumb on top grip
- ☐ Rotate your hand and forearm to the horizontal position, your palm is up toward the sky
- ☐ Elbow is close to your side
- ☐ Begin the cast (either back or forward) using just your rod hand

Photo 55-rod arm turned horizontal

Back cast:

- ☐ Start with a bent down wrist and the rod butt parallel to forearm
- ☐ Move your rod hand toward the back cast target
- ☐ Move your entire forearm and wrist together to get the line, leader and fly moving as a unit and lined up with your back cast target
- ☐ Watch the rod begin to bend, or load
- ☐ Use your thumb to aim the back cast
- ☐ When thumbnail is lined up opposite the back cast target, begin the wrist rotation
- ☐ Squeeze the rod butt and tighten your arm muscles to make the stop
- ☐ The wrist will change to the straight position and the rod butt is now at 45° angle
- ☐ After the stop move your eyes to the rod tip: watch the loop form and unroll to your target
- ☐ Allow the cast to fall and evaluate your cast
- ☐ Evaluate the stroke length, power and speed
- ☐ Check your wrist position

Photo 56-start horizontal casting

Photo series 52- top: stop position, note rod is perpendicular to target; bottom: optional drift move, note elbow leaves side and wrist is straight position

Photo series 53- top: forward cast start position; bottom: forward cast to target, wrist in bent down position

Forward cast:

☐ Forearm and hand rotated to the horizontal position
☐ Start with the wrist in the straight position
☐ Move your entire forearm and wrist together to get the line, leader and fly moving as a unit and lined up with your forward cast target
☐ Watch the rod begin to bend, or load
☐ Use your thumb to aim the cast
☐ When thumb pad is lined up opposite the forward cast target, begin the wrist rotation
☐ Push forward with the thumb while pulling back with the lower fingers
☐ Wrist is in the bent down position
☐ Rod butt moves to be parallel with forearm
☐ After the stop move your eyes to the rod tip: watch the loop form and unroll to your target
☐ Allow the cast to fall and evaluate the cast
☐ Evaluate the stroke length, power and speed
☐ Check your wrist position

Continue using the rod hand only and allowing each cast to fall. Cast slowly to watch your rod arm move through the casting stroke. After isolating the cast, make a back cast and forward cast together. Be sure your forearm and hand stay in the horizontal position and does not dip or roll during the casting stroke. Start by making just one complete false cast. Next, make a series of 3-4 false casts, always evaluating the cast and your rod arm mechanics. Once you feel confident with false casting, close your eyes and concentrate on the feeling in your hand. Feel the rod movement through the stroke and the loading and unloading of the rod.

Complete your practice session by changing the casting plane. Bring your rod up from horizontal to off vertical, at the one o'clock angle. Make a few false casts in this plane. You should now have a mental picture of what is happening while you are casting. Present your cast and relax.

When ready, use this exercise with to practice the double haul.

Casting Form

It is helpful to identify the parts of the casting stroke, and the series of movements to make the cast. It can be difficult to understand the importance of the loading before you start the wrist rotation on the stop. Using a casting form with the horizontal casting exercise helps identify the parts of the cast and allows you to see how your movements contribute to making the cast. The form gives you parameters for the loading move and stops. It helps you see where the wrist rotation occurs in the stroke. When you add drift and follow through, the casting form can help you find exactly where in the cast these occur.

Key concepts:
- The form identifies the parts of the cast
- The center dowels identify the space in the casting stroke for the wrist rotation to occur
- Wrist rotation occurs over a few inches, as you rotate to the stop
- The loading movement positions the rod for the stop and wrist rotation
- The loading must occur before the wrist rotation
- The outer dowels identifying the positions for drift and follow through
- The drift space serves as the space for the next forward cast loading
- The follow through space serves as the space for next back cast loading
- The elbow moves away from the body of drift and follow through
- The elbow is close to the body at the stop positions
- Use with the horizontal casting exercise, on grass

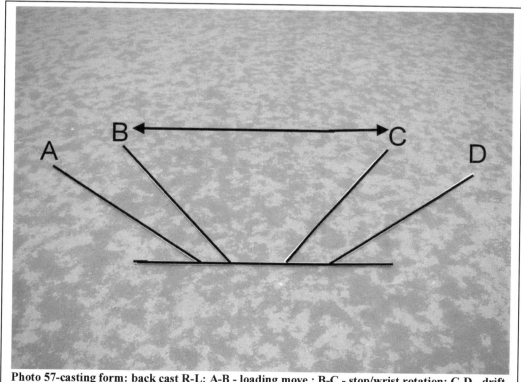

Photo 57-casting form: <u>**back cast**</u> **R-L: A-B - loading move ; B-C - stop/wrist rotation; C-D - drift** <u>**forward cast**</u>**: L-R: D-C- loading move; C-B- stop/wrist rotation; B-A-follow through**

Set up:
- ☐ Use four dowels of 3-4 feet in length, the set up for this exercise is similar to the horizontal casting exercise
- ☐ Use 30 feet of fly line
- ☐ Place the rod on the ground and position the line out of the rod tip at a right angle
- ☐ Extend the line so it is straight
- ☐ Place a target a foot or two beyond the yarn fly
- ☐ Use a three foot round target
- ☐ Walk the fly line to the other side of the rod, again creating a right angle from the rod tip
- ☐ Extend the line so it is straight, place the second target a foot or two beyond the yarn fly
- ☐ Both targets should be in line with your rod tip
- ☐ Place a 6 foot piece of rope, or yarn just below your rod butt to create a straight line for your base on the form
- ☐ Keeping your rod in the center, place a dowel on either side of the rod
- ☐ Place dowels approximately 12 inches apart, approximately at 45°angle to the straight line base, this marks the wrist rotation part of the cast
- ☐ Start with just two dowels to focus on the stops and wrist rotation (positions B-C)
- ☐ Add an additional dowel 18 inches to right and left of the original dowel at a 30° angle to the baseline, this identifies drift and follow through (D & A)

Casting form exercise:
- ☐ Stand sideways to the targets, facing the dowels
- ☐ Hold the rod with your usual thumb on top grip
- ☐ Rotate your hand and forearm to the horizontal casting position
- ☐ Use the rod hand only
- ☐ Begin with a back cast

Back cast:
- ☐ Wrist in the bent down position
- ☐ Move your forearm and hand horizontally until your thumbnail is positioned directly opposite your back cast target, your rod hand should be over the first dowel (B)
- ☐ At the stop, squeeze the rod butt as the wrist moves to the straight position, during the stroke
- ☐ When the stop is complete, your hand should be at the dowel to you right (C)
- ☐ The wrist rotation occurs over a few inches, which helps apply the power smoothly
- ☐ Allow the cast to fall and evaluate the cast
- ☐ If using drift, move the rod to the drift position after the stop (D)
- ☐ Use this space to load the rod on the next forward cast (D-C)
- ☐ Elbow leaves your side during drift
- ☐ Elbow returns to your side as you begin the next forward cast

184

Forward cast:
- ☐ Wrist in the straight position
- ☐ Move your forearm and hand horizontally until your thumbnail is positioned directly opposite your forward cast target (D-C)
- ☐ At the stop position, push forward with the thumb and pulling back with the lower fingers as the wrist rotates to the bent down position, during the stroke
- ☐ When the stop is complete, your hand should be at the dowel on your left (B)
- ☐ The wrist rotation occurs over a few inches, which helps apply the power smoothly
- ☐ Allow the cast to fall and evaluate the cast
- ☐ If using follow through, move the rod to the follow through position after the stop (A)
- ☐ Use this space to load the rod on the next back cast (A-B)
- ☐ Elbow leaves your side during follow through
- ☐ Elbow moves back to your side as you begin the next back cast

Once you are comfortable with the using the form with each cast, begin false casting with the form. You will find that these dowels represent the casting arc. Using this form can help you see the casting arc needed for straight line casting with this length of line. The exact stroke length and casting arc will vary with the length of line being cast. Use the above set up as a guideline. Increase the casting arc for longer lengths of line and tighten the arc for shorter lengths of line. With a very short line, you will need a minimal loading move. The cast will be mostly the wrist rotation.

Start with the basic form, using just two dowels to focus on the stop positions and wrist rotation. Add the two additional dowels to represent drift and follow through. This will help you connect the feeling of drift and follow through with their place in the casting stroke. As you false cast watch for your forearm to move horizontally across the form. The elbow moves away from the body on drift and follow through, returning during the acceleration (loading move) and stop. False cast for short time periods as this position can be fatiguing.

Visual Straight Line Casting

The horizontal casting exercise combined with a visual line helps to improve your ability to cast along a straight line. Set up for horizontal casting as usual. Use a straight line, which is painted on an athletic field, or a rope that is placed between your two targets. You will use the straight line at your rod tip as a guide for the straight line path.

Key concepts:
- Using a visual straight line facilitates the straight line path movement of your rod arm
- Drift and follow through occur along the straight line
- Focus on the rod tip moving along the rope
- Elbow leaves your side on drift and follow through
- Elbow is close to your side on the stop positions
- Horizontal casting allows you to watch the cast

Straight line exercise:
Set Up: Similar to horizontal casting, with a rope between the targets
- ☐ Back cast
  - o Starts with rod arm extend slightly to the left
  - o Elbow moves back toward body at beginning of casting stroke
  - o Rod tip moves along the rope
  - o Elbow is close to your side during the stop
- ☐ Drift: occurs after the stop
  - o Repositions the rod tip along the straight line path (maintains the loop shape)
- ☐ Forward cast
  - o Begins with elbow returning toward your side
  - o Rod tip moves along the rope during the casting stroke
  - o Elbow is close to your side on the stop
- ☐ Follow through: occurs after the stop
  - o Repositions the rod tip forward, along the straight line to maintain the loop shape
- ☐ False casting
  - o Elbow moves to facilitate the straight line path of the rod tip
    - ▪ Elbow must move away from your body on drift and follow through
    - ▪ Elbow is close to your side during the stops
    - ▪ Elbow returns close to your body on the loading move in both directions
- ☐ Casting arc
  - o Watch the stop position of the rod butt on both back cast and forward cast
  - o These stop positions show you the casting arc
  - o Too wide an arc yields a wide loop
  - o Too narrow an arc yields a closed, tailing loop

Make a series of back and forward casts. Move through the casting stroke slowly so you can focus on the path your rod arm takes to maintain the rod tip along the straight line. Notice that if you move too close the straight line your cast will be above the line. In order to cast along the straight line you must stand about a rod length away from the rope. False cast a series of 3-4 false casts. First focusing on the rod tip moving along the straight line and then how your rod arm moves to ensure this straight line path. Remember to check your rod butt to forearm and wrist positions at the beginning and end of each cast.

Photo 58-straight line rope with 2 targets

Two Straight Lines

Another variation of horizontal casting exercise is to use two straight lines. This allows you focus on the tracking of your cast. Tracking is your ability to cast in a straight line front to back, with no lateral or side to side deviation. If you do not track straight, you may have a slice, or angle to your target. When casting distance, your errors are magnified the further the distance you cast. If you are just one degree off on your tracking to a target at 60 feet, you may miss your target by 3 feet. The same one-degree tracking error for a target at 85 feet may result in your fly being 10 feet off target. You need to track straight to the target to be accurate and efficient. Think of a set of train tracks that keep the train straight, with no side-to-side deviation. Using two ropes, you can cast within these ropes to be certain you are tracking straight. Watch your loops as you cast to be sure they are within the boundaries of the ropes. Using two ropes can also help you monitor tracking and loop size when casting at different angles.

Key concepts:
- Using two visual straight lines simulates a "track" for your cast, provides boundaries for the cast
- Goal is to cast straight to each target, no lateral deviation
- Drift and follow through occur within the boundaries of the ropes
- Loop should unroll within the two ropes
- Horizontal casting allows you to watch the cast, including drift and follow through
- Focus on tracking as you cast at different angles

Photo 59-- 2 straight lines with targets

<u>Two Straight lines exercise</u>:

Set up: Similar to horizontal casting, place two ropes approximately 5 feet apart, Place the back cast and forward cast targets near the end, between the two ropes.

- ☐ Back cast
  - ○ Stand sideways, midway along the ropes
  - ○ Rod tip just inside the rope closest to you
  - ○ Start with rod arm extend slightly to the left
  - ○ Elbow moves toward body at beginning of casting stroke
  - ○ Rod tip moves along close to the lower rope
  - ○ Elbow is close to your side during the stop
- ☐ Drift: occurs after the stop
  - ○ Repositions the rod tip along the straight line path
  - ○ Direction of drift maintains the loop shape
  - ○ Loop unrolls between the two ropes
- ☐ Forward cast
  - ○ Begins with elbow returning toward your side
  - ○ Rod tip moves close to the lower rope during the casting stroke
  - ○ Elbow is close to your side on the stop
- ☐ Follow through: occurs after the stop
  - ○ Repositions the rod tip forward
  - ○ Direction of follow through maintains the loop shape
  - ○ Loop unrolls between the two ropes
- ☐ False casting
  - ○ Casting loops unroll within the ropes both back and forward cast
  - ○ Loops unroll directly over the targets
  - ○ Elbow moves to facilitate the straight line path of the rod tip
    - ▪ Elbow must move away from your body on drift and follow through
    - ▪ Elbow is close to your side during the stops

As you practice with the two ropes, you can use different casting planes including the off shoulder planes. You will need to adjust your distance to the ropes to be sure the loops unroll within the rope boundaries.

Back Cast Aiming

To make a good, straight line back cast, it is helpful to develop the habit of aiming your back cast. Isolate your back cast and practice a series of back casts. Begin by casting in the vertical plane and make your back cast to unroll over an object. Find a small tree, large bush or a short fence, stand in front of this object and cast over the object (you will need to be sure your fly line does not get tangled in the object). With off vertical angles select an object which matches the height of your casting angle. If casting horizontally aim your back cast to land under a low hanging branch or over a bucket. You can also use the bleacher seats at an athletic field to cast at a 45° angle. Aim your cast to go over a bench about halfway up the bleacher. To cast at a 30°angle aim your cast at the top of the home plate backstop. Do not allow your fly line to land on the target as it may tangle. Use the object as the aiming point. Watch your cast to see if it would likely have hit the target.

Key concepts:
- Back cast trajectory is a straight line cast
- Selecting a back cast target facilitates this straight line
- Use targets at various heights, look for targets in the practice area: shrub, fence, light pole
- Practice different casting planes
- Use the open stance so you can look at your target
- Looking at the target area improves aiming
- Maximum back cast stop position is forearm to upper arm: use body structure to stop the rod

<u>Back cast aiming practice checklist</u>
- ☐ Start with the line out straight in front of you and no slack line
- ☐ Start in the vertical position, this requires a high target level such as a cloud
- ☐ Look at your back cast target and aim your cast
- ☐ Move rod arm on a straight line to the target
- ☐ Make the back cast then turn your head to look up and watch the loop unroll
- ☐ Back cast should unroll directly in line with your target, and at the appropriate height
- ☐ Allow cast to fall and evaluate the cast

- ☐ Use the open stance and cast at an off vertical angle
- ☐ Select a target at low, medium and high angles
- ☐ Look at your back cast target and aim the cast
- ☐ Move rod arm on a straight line to the target
- ☐ Make your back cast and watch the loop unroll
- ☐ Back cast should unroll directly in line with your target, at the appropriate height and casting angle
- ☐ Allow the cast to fall and evaluate
- ☐ Make a forward cast to straighten line and repeat the back cast

Use the isolating the cast exercise, to practice a series of back casts.

Photo 60- practice aiming back cast low, mid and high relative to a target

Continuous False Casting

Making a long series of false casts provides you the opportunity to evaluate the loop and make immediate corrections. The danger is that when making a long series of false casts, it is easy to allow the rhythm of the casting sequence take over and control the cast. You can develop a rhythm that perpetuates itself, but is not related to the specific cast. Your goal is to develop a heightened sense of awareness for each cast, including awareness of corrections and their results. When continuously casting, you need to be sure that your rod hand and arm do not remain tense throughout the cast. Tension impedes your ability to feel the cast and the subtle nuances of changes in the interaction of the line and rod as it loads and unloads. Limit your continuous casting to include a series of 6-8 casts. This will help avoid muscle fatigue and keep you focused.

Continuously false casting helps you to develop rod arm strength and allows you to focus on tracking. You can work on aiming, and incorporating drift and follow through with false casting. Remember to use hand and arm tension only on the stops and relaxing during the remainder of the cast.

Continuous double hauling helps you to monitor your line hand for slack, and match the length and speed of your hauls to your cast. Focus on the direction of the hauls and the timing of the giving back of line. By making an extended series of double hauls, you have time for the feedback and correction mechanisms to occur.

The One Cast

In contrast to continuous casting is the one cast. In this case, you have only one opportunity to get the cast perfect. The value is that you have a more focused concentration for that single cast. When the cast ends, it is easy to recall the feeling of that cast and connect your feeling to the outcome. The one cast exercise uses a complete cast (back cast and forward cast), and may include shooting line, or the double haul. The sequence is to start with your line out straight in front of you; make a back cast followed by the forward delivery cast; stop and evaluate the cast. The variations are to add the double haul, and to shoot line on the back cast. Each cast involves a single back cast followed by a delivery cast. This single, complete cast helps you work on the back cast timing: starting the forward cast just as the back cast is straight behind you. This is a great way to practice timing and concentrate on the feeling in the rod as you progressively load the rod. This exercise will also help you to slow down and not rush through the forward delivery cast. It does not allow you to anticipate the delivery cast and eliminates your desire to put extra power into this cast. I find this a very humbling exercise to trying to be precise with only one chance.

Advanced Casting Techniques: Lesson 2: Intermediate Fly Casting

Practice for the intermediate and advanced caster uses many of the same exercises. The main difference between the intermediate and advanced caster's practice is in the level of detail. The intermediate caster seeks improvement from the beginner level skill set. Their focus is improvement of the basic skills and developing new techniques like the double haul. Generally, their goal is to fish in more challenging conditions. The advanced caster has accomplished many skills but needs to focus on refinement of these skills in order to get the improvement desired. Generally, the advanced caster has been fishing for a long time and has adapted their casting habits to compensate for basic flaws. Their flaws only show up as they push the limits of their capabilities. The advanced caster generally needs to focus on the minute details in their cast. They are already casting well enough but to get their casting to the" next level" they need to refine the basics.

This section presents a series of casting exercises. These exercises are for all levels of casters. Use these exercises to help you develop and refine your casting techniques.

Casting techniques:
- ☐ The five essentials
- ☐ Wind
- ☐ Accuracy
- ☐ Hauls: double and single
- ☐ Shooting line efficiently
- ☐ Drift
- ☐ Rod arm mechanics: off vertical & drift
- ☐ Longer casting stroke
- ☐ Casting arc

The Five Essentials

As you begin to practice your casting, you can start by focusing on the five essential elements of a good straight line cast. Keep these elements in mind as you use any of the casting exercises. The casting exercises are techniques to help you identify which of the elements is damaging your cast. It is common to violate more than one element at time. One bad move generally creates a compensatory move, so you may have multiple areas to improve. As you practice, focus on improving one essential at a time. Apply the five essentials to each cast, back and forward, and then to your false casting.

Key concepts:
- There are 5 essentials elements to make a good straight line cast
- Violating any one of these elements will damage the cast
- The essentials incorporate the factors which vary with increasing distance
- Provides a good starting point for evaluating and improving your cast
- Improvement is focused on substantive areas
- Allows for variations in style of how the cast is executed

The Five Essentials:
1. Slack line is kept to a minimum
2. Straight line path of the rod tip
3. Casting stroke starts slowly and is an overall acceleration to an abrupt stop (includes a loading move then a wrist rotation on the stop)
4. Power must be applied smoothly and gradually
5. The casting stroke length and casting arc must vary in proportion to the length of line being cast

Essential	Key concept
1. Slack line is kept to a minimum	Maintain the fly line under tension and a bend in the rod
2. Straight line path of the rod tip	Move the rod on a straight line during both the back and forward casts
3. Casting stroke starts slowly and is an overall acceleration to an abrupt stop	Start the loading of the rod gradually, through acceleration you deepen the rod bend, then unload the rod with an abrupt stop
4. Power must be applied smoothly and gradually	Do not force your strength on the rod, work with the rod to pull it into a bend, no "hitting" the cast
5. The casting stroke length and casting arc must vary in proportion to the length of line being cast	Short cast-short stroke-narrow arc; long cast-long stroke-wide arc; add drift and follow through forward as you increase the length of line being cast

Five Essential Elements
Back cast: use with isolating the cast exercise

Start with rod tip low	Slack line is kept to a minimum
Aim your back cast on a diagonal straight line behind you, cast in the vertical position to aim back cast up behind you	Straight line path of the rod tip
Begin the casting stroke slowly, watch the line as it leaves the water, look for minimal disturbance	Casting stroke starts slowly and is an overall acceleration to an abrupt stop
Smoothly accelerate the rod to your stop position, no hesitation in the stroke	Power must be applied smoothly and gradually
Back cast ends when you reach the line-leader connection on the lift, add drift for distance casting	The casting stroke length and casting arc must vary in proportion to the length of line being cast

Forward cast: use with isolating the cast exercise

Start forward just as the loop of line straightens behind you	Slack line is kept to a minimum
Aim your forward cast for the correct trajectory toward your target, be sure to incorporate the stop on this straight line	Straight line path of the rod tip
Begin the forward cast slowly: leading with the elbow and finishing with the hand	Casting stroke starts slowly and is an overall acceleration to an abrupt stop
Build acceleration gradually, wrist rotation on the stop is smooth, in a forward projection	Power must be applied smoothly and gradually
Add follow through forward for a longer cast, and use a more narrow casting arc, tilted downward for shorter casts	The casting stroke length and casting arc must vary in proportion to the length of line being cast

False casting: use with continuous false casting exercise

Each cast uses just enough speed and power to keep it aloft	Slack line is kept to a minimum
Be sure you are casting in a straight line by using targets	Straight line path of the rod tip
Start each cast slowly and accelerate to the stop	Casting stroke starts slowly and is an overall acceleration to an abrupt stop
Watch for extra wiggles in your loop that signals excess power or speed	Power must be applied smoothly and gradually
Increase the stroke length and casting arc for longer casts, decrease the stroke length and casting arc for shorter casts	The casting stroke length and casting arc must vary in proportion to the length of line being cast

Wind

Practice with winds from all directions and be sure to use targets so your accuracy improves.

Key concepts:
- Determine the effects of the wind on your line and fly
- Make adjustments to counteract the effect of the wind
- Change the casting plane, trajectory, timing or line placement
- High line speed to cut through the wind
- Tight loops are more aerodynamic
- Use hauls (double or single) as appropriate

Wind practice
- ☐ Headwind problem: difficult to unroll the forward cast
  - o Horizontal casting: low profile to the wind
  - o High back cast with low forward cast: change in trajectory, do not stop beyond 12 o'clock on back cast and unroll forward cast just above the target
- ☐ Tailwind problem: back cast cannot straighten, so poor set up for forward cast
  - o Adjust timing: do not wait back cast to unroll, start forward cast sooner
  - o Aim forward cast high so wind the helps the cast unroll: change trajectory
  - o Use two forward casts: using your strength to make the cast
    - ▪ Stand sideways to the target
    - ▪ False cast away from target (target on left, false cast to right)
    - ▪ While false cast unrolls, rotate hand and forearm to position for forward cast (to left)
    - ▪ Begin forward casting stroke in the new direction (left)
    - ▪ Make the delivery cast
- ☐ Rod arm wind problem: line blown into the caster
  - o Horizontal casting: a change in trajectory for low profile to the wind
  - o Off shoulder casting: line placement change to the downwind side
  - o Present on your back cast: line placement change, uses wind to help you cast
    - ▪ Stand sideways to target
    - ▪ False cast away from the target area
    - ▪ After the back cast stop, allow the cast to fall and fish this cast
- ☐ Line hand wind problem: cast blown downwind from target
  - o Cast upwind of target and adjust aiming for accuracy

Practice wind techniques using these practice exercises:
- Complete back and forward cast
- Horizontal casting
- Drift time to change direction (two forward casts)
- Casting in all planes: side arm and off shoulder casting angles
- Two straight lines for off shoulder accuracy
- Aiming the back cast
- Accuracy

Accuracy

Accuracy is controlling the placement of your fly. In order to be successful in fly casting you must be able to place your fly exactly where you want it. To practice accuracy, use multiple targets. Several Frisbees work well. Place the targets at varied distances and angles from where you are standing. Be sure to place some targets behind you to practice for the unexpected fish presenting from behind.

Key concepts:
The smaller the target area and the further the distance to the target, the more difficult it is to be accurate.
- Always cast with targets
- Accuracy has two dimensions: distance to target and lateral(side to side) accuracy
- The principles of accuracy involve two imaginary straight lines
- Eye-target line is imaginary straight line from your eye to your target
- Hand-target line is an imaginary straight line from your rod hand to the target
- Use your thumb as an aiming device
- Thumb pad in forward direction and thumbnail in back cast direction
- Hand-target line intersects the eye-target line at the target
- Keep rod hand and thumb close to eyes to facilitating accuracy
- Bend at the waist for horizontal casting: hand-target and eye-target lines are closer and facilitate accuracy
- Use horizontal plane to accurately present the fly to a target behind you

Accuracy practice set up:
- ☐ Place your targets at random angles and distances
- ☐ Begin with false casting
- ☐ Aim your cast to unroll a few feet above your target
- ☐ Watch your yarn fly unroll well above the target
- ☐ Evaluate for distance and lateral accuracy
- ☐ Adjust line by shooting or stripping in line, for the correct distance
- ☐ Adjust your rod arm path for aiming at center of the target
- ☐ Aim your cast to unroll just above the target
- ☐ Deliver your fly, allow the cast to land and evaluate your accuracy
- ☐ Repeat this procedure at a new target and distance
- ☐ Practice your accuracy in the wind from all directions (incorporate wind practice information)
- ☐ Practice accuracy on your off shoulder side
  - o Change stance
  - o Be sure hand is in front of face
- ☐ Present the fly accurately at a target behind you
  - o Stand sideways to target
  - o Use the horizontal casting plane

Practice accuracy techniques using these practice exercises:
- Isolating the back and forward cast
- Aiming the back cast
- Horizontal casting
- Straight line casting with visual line
- Rod arm mechanics
- Wrist rotation practice

Photo series 54- coordinate eye-target and hand-target lines in all planes

Hauls: Double and Single

Hauling is complex because during the haul, your line hand and rod hand move in opposite directions. Everyone needs to practice the hauls; they just do not come naturally. There are several options for practicing the hauls: focusing on just the haul; practicing the haul and give back on a single cast in the horizontal position; or by using water and hauling on the back cast pick up. Try all of these exercises and see which helps you the most.

Key concepts:
- Double haul is a haul and give back: a two direction move
- Single haul is a one direction move: a haul with no give back
- Haul is coordinated with the wrist action on the stop
- Length of the haul is matched to the length of the wrist rotation
- Haul is balanced to the cast for speed and power
- Direction of the haul is opposite the rod's movement
- Haul accelerates to a stop, it is a crisp, sharp move
- The give back motion is slower, at the rate the unrolling loop will accept the line
- Line hand must be sure there is no slack line
- Monitor the line from the first stripping guide to the line hand; this should always be under tension
- Haul will increase line speed, deepen the load in the rod and form a tighter loop

Line hand: Haul movement practice:
Set up:
- ☐ Use 40 feet of line
- ☐ Place two equidistant targets on the ground, similar to the set up for horizontal casting exercise
- ☐ Place the rod under your armpit and wrap your forearm around the rod so it rests in the bend of your elbow
- ☐ Hold the rod shaft with your lower fingers
- ☐ Stand between the targets so one is on each side of you
- ☐ Use body motion to move and stop the rod by swinging side to side

False casting
- ☐ Use body motion to move the rod, swing right to left and back right to left, simulating a back cast and forward cast
- ☐ Your hips and shoulders swing side to side
- ☐ After each swing to a side, pause to allow the loop to unroll
- ☐ Watch the loop unroll over your target
- ☐ Now add your line hand to haul and give back on each cast
- ☐ Keep the line in the air, false casting as you haul and give back
- ☐ Watch the line from the first stripping guide to your line hand to be sure there is no slack line.
- ☐ Make 6-8 false casts with double hauls and then rest

Photo 61-use body to swing rod while false casting, focus on haul hand functions

<u>Double Haul on the grass</u>: Horizontal casting to practice your double haul

Set up:
- ☐ Set up is identical to horizontal casting exercise
- ☐ Be sure to use targets that are placed 180° from each other
- ☐ Use 40 feet of line
- ☐ Allow 2-3 feet of line between your hands so you have line to use for hauling

Back cast:
- ☐ Start with wrist bent down and the rod butt parallel to forearm
- ☐ Line hand palm is down, yet parallel with rod hand
- ☐ Move your line hand and rod hand in unison toward your back cast target
- ☐ Watch the rod begin to bend, or load
- ☐ Use your rod arm thumb to aim the back cast
- ☐ When thumbnail is lined up opposite the back cast target, begin the wrist rotation of the stop
- ☐ The line hand hauls **while** the rod hand executes the stop
- ☐ Line hand accelerates to the left, opposite the rod hand movement
- ☐ Wrist changes to the straight position, rod butt is at 45° angle **and** the haul has ended
- ☐ After the rod stop, move your eyes to the line hand and watch the line to ensure tension as you perform the give back
- ☐ Line hand returns to its position slightly below the reel
- ☐ Allow the cast to fall and evaluate your haul and give back
- ☐ Rest your arm

Forward cast:
- ☐ Rotate rod arm and line hand to the horizontal position
- ☐ Rod hand wrist is in the straight position (45°angle)
- ☐ Line hand palm is down, and parallel with rod hand
- ☐ Move your line hand and rod hand in unison toward your forward cast target
- ☐ Watch the rod begin to bend
- ☐ Use your thumb to aim the cast
- ☐ When thumb pad is lined up opposite the forward cast target, begin the wrist rotation
- ☐ The line hand hauls **while** the rod hand executes the stop
- ☐ Line hand accelerates toward left hip, opposite the rod hand movement
- ☐ The wrist changes to the bent down position, **and** the haul has ended
- ☐ After the rod stop, move your eyes to the line hand and watch the line for tension as you give back
- ☐ Line hand returns to just below the reel
- ☐ Allow the cast to fall and evaluate your haul and give back
- ☐ Rest your arm

After you have practiced single back and forward casts, false cast with double hauling. Monitor the line in your line hand to be sure there is no slack line. Watch the loop as it unrolls and give the line back at the rate the unrolling loop will accept. Close your eyes, feel the haul, and give back. Feel the line under tension. Open your eyes and move to the vertical position. Make six false casts with double hauling and then rest.

Photo series 55- top: hands start together while loading the rod; mid: hands separate on the stop; bottom: line hand gives back as loop accepts the line

Photo series 56- top: start of forward cast haul; bottom: forward haul completed

Double Haul off the water

Set up:
- ☐ Use a pond for practice
- ☐ Use 40 feet of line
- ☐ Allow 2-3 feet of line between hands so you have line to use for hauling
- ☐ Line hand and rod hand should be slightly separated to keep line from tangling on the reel
- ☐ Start in the vertical position

Back cast:
- ☐ Roll cast to straighten the line
- ☐ Start with a bent down wrist, rod butt parallel to forearm
- ☐ Line hand pinching fly line, positioned a few inches away, but in parallel with rod hand
- ☐ Move line hand and rod hand in unison for the back cast
- ☐ Watch your line as you lift it off the water
- ☐ When you reach the line-leader connection, the line hand hauls **while** the rod hand executes the stop
- ☐ Line hand accelerates forward, opposite the rod hand movement
- ☐ The wrist changes to the straight position, rod butt is now at a 45° angle **and** the haul has ended
- ☐ After the rod stop, move your eyes to the line hand and watch the line for tension as you give back line
- ☐ Line hand moves to give back line, positioning the line hand just below the reel (prevent tangles)
- ☐ Make the forward cast, with or without a double haul

Forward cast:
- ☐ Rod hand wrist in the straight position (45°angle)
- ☐ Line hand pinching fly line is positioned just below the reel
- ☐ Rod hand and line hand move in unison for the forward cast
- ☐ Use the rod hand thumb to aim the cast
- ☐ When thumb pad is lined up opposite the forward cast target, begin the wrist rotation
- ☐ The line hand hauls **while** the rod hand executes the stop
- ☐ Line hand accelerates back, toward your left hip, opposite the rod hand movement
- ☐ The wrist changes to the bent down position, **and** the haul has ended
- ☐ After the rod stop, move your eyes to the line hand and watch the line for tension as you give back line
- ☐ Line hand returns to just below the reel
- ☐ Allow the cast to fall and evaluate your haul and give back
- ☐ Rest your arm

Using the double haul off water is especially helpful for learning the back cast double haul. You can double haul on just the back cast or both casts. On the forward cast, it can be helpful to think of the hauling to help the rod tip move through the apex of the bend (loaded rod). When you feel comfortable double hauling on each cast, combine false casting with the double haul. Make six false casts and double hauls then present the cast.

Photo series 57- top: hands start the cast in same direction; bottom: haul is timed with fly leaving the water on the stop

<u>Single Hauls practice</u>
Key concepts:
- Single haul is a one direction movement
- Haul without a give back of the line
- Used with strong winds
- Single haul on the back cast with a strong tailwind
- Single haul on the forward cast with a headwind
- Use two single hauls for tailwind that also requires high line speed on the forward delivery cast
  - Haul hand should not fully extend
  - Line hand maintains a bend in the elbow, at the end of the haul
  - Line hand pivots, maintaining its relationship to rod hand during the forward cast loading
- Direction of hauls are the same as for double haul, opposite the rod arm movement

Set up:
- ☐ Use 40 feet of line
- ☐ Allow 2-3 feet of line between hands so you have line to use for hauling
- ☐ Line hand and rod hand should be slightly separated to keep line from tangling on the reel
- ☐ Start in the vertical position
- ☐ Use a pond or grass field

<u>Back cast single haul</u>
Back cast:
- ☐ Start with a bent down wrist, rod butt is parallel to forearm
- ☐ Line hand pinching fly line is positioned a few inches away, but is parallel with the rod hand
- ☐ Move line hand and rod hand in unison for the back cast (loading move)
- ☐ Watch your line as you lift it off the water
- ☐ When you reach the line-leader connection, the line hand hauls **while** the rod hand executes the stop
- ☐ Line hand accelerates forward, hauling opposite the rod hand movement
- ☐ Wrist changes to the straight position, rod butt is now at a 45° angle **and** the haul has ended
- ☐ Line hand has a bend in the elbow
- ☐ Line hand maintains its position while the loop unrolls

Forward cast
- ☐ Rod hand wrist in the straight position (45°angle)
- ☐ Line hand maintains its position at the end of the haul
- ☐ Line hand **pivots** while rod hand moves for the forward cast (during loading)
- ☐ Use the rod hand thumb to aim the cast
- ☐ When thumb pad is lined up opposite the target, begin the wrist rotation of the stop
- ☐ Rod hand executes the stop
- ☐ Line hand either releases the line for shooting or continues holding the line
- ☐ Line hand traps the line under middle finger of rod hand for fishing

Photo series 58- back cast single haul, line hand holds its position after haul, elbow is bent, line hand pivots through forward cast

Forward cast single haul

Back cast:

- ☐ Start with a bent down wrist, rod butt parallel to forearm
- ☐ Line hand pinching fly line, positioned a few inches away, but is parallel with rod hand
- ☐ Move line hand and rod hand in unison for the back cast
- ☐ Watch your line as you lift it off the water
- ☐ When you reach the line-leader connection, the wrist changes to the straight position, rod butt is now at a 45° angle
- ☐ Line hand has a bend in the elbow
- ☐ Line hand maintains its position just below the reel

Forward cast

- ☐ Rod hand wrist is in the straight position (45°angle)
- ☐ Line hand maintains its position
- ☐ Rod hand and line hand move in unison for the forward cast
- ☐ Use the rod hand thumb to aim the cast
- ☐ When thumb pad is lined up opposite the forward cast target, begin the wrist rotation
- ☐ The line hand hauls **while** the rod hand executes the stop
- ☐ Line hand accelerates back, toward your left hip, opposite the rod hand movement
- ☐ Wrist changes to the bent down position, **and** the haul has ended
- ☐ After the rod stops, you can release the line for shooting

Photo series 59- forward cast single haul, hands start the casting stroke together and separate on the stop

<u>Two Single Hauls</u>:

Back cast

- ☐ Start with a bent down wrist, rod butt parallel to forearm
- ☐ Line hand pinching fly line, positioned a few inches away, but in parallel with rod hand
- ☐ Move line hand and rod hand in unison for the back cast
- ☐ Watch your line as you lift it off the water
- ☐ When you reach the line-leader connection, the line hand hauls **while** the rod hand executes the stop
- ☐ Line hand accelerates forward, hauling opposite the rod hand movement
- ☐ Wrist changes to the straight position, rod butt is now at a 45° angle **and** the haul has ended
- ☐ Line hand has a bend in the elbow
- ☐ Line hand maintains its position while the loop unrolls

Forward cast

- ☐ Rod hand wrist in the straight position (45°angle)
- ☐ Line hand maintains its position at the end of the haul
- ☐ Line hand **pivots** while rod hand moves for the forward cast (loading move)
- ☐ Use the rod hand thumb to aim the cast
- ☐ When thumb pad is lined up opposite the forward cast target, begin the wrist rotation
- ☐ Line hand performs the second haul **while** the rod hand executes the stop
- ☐ Line hand accelerates back, toward your left hip, opposite the rod hand movement
- ☐ Wrist changes to the bent down position, **and** the haul has ended
- ☐ After the rod stops, you can give back the line or release for shooting

Practice hauling techniques using these practice exercises:

- • Horizontal casting and its variations
- • Isolating each cast
- • Practice in both vertical and off vertical casting planes

Shooting Line Efficiently

To eliminate excessive false casting and maximize you cast, you need to plan your sequence for false casting and shooting line. Understanding your fly line design helps you to maximize your plan for casting and shooting line.

Key concepts:
- Line can be shot on forward or back cast
- Need line outside of the rod tip to provide weight to pull additional line with the shoot
- Line being shot is pulled by the energy in the loop of fly line
- Efficient unloading of the rod provides energy in the loop
- Loop must form before you shoot line
- Line hand alternately pinches and releases the line
- Maximum line shoot is determined by the casters ability to control the line, and the line design (avoid excess overhang)
- Minimize false casting and plan the line shoot

Set up:
- ☐ Start with 40 feet of line (40 foot line marking in your hand)
- ☐ Strip off an additional 10 feet of line for shooting
- ☐ Be sure the line is stretched to remove coils

Back cast
- ☐ Use either closed or open stance
- ☐ Use rod hand and line hand
- ☐ Start with line straight in front of you
- ☐ Make a back cast
- ☐ Focus on the abrupt stop
- ☐ After the back cast stop, while the loop is unrolling, shoot a few inches of line
- ☐ Pinch the line to stop the shoot
- ☐ Allow the loop to almost unroll
- ☐ Begin the forward cast

Forward cast
- ☐ Continue the forward casting stroke
- ☐ Aim the forward cast
- ☐ When thumb pad is opposite the forward cast target area, begin the wrist rotation of the stop
- ☐ Watch for the loop to form
- ☐ Release line and shoot a few inches
- ☐ Pinch the line to stop the shoot
- ☐ Allow loop to unroll and for the deliver cast

When comfortable with pinching and releasing the line, try false casting with the line shoot. Practice shooting line on each cast. Avoid excessive false casting and shooting line.

Do not exceed your ability to control the line. Efficient line shooting involves planning the amount of line to be shot, and when in the false casting sequence you plan to shoot.

Practice shooting line techniques using these practice exercises:

- Isolating each cast
- Horizontal casting

Photo 62- line hand forms a circle and controls the shoot

Drift

Drift gives you the feeling of constant tension on the line. It allows you to stay in contact with the line as it unrolls. Drift is a repositioning of the rod tip after the stop. You can drift back for a longer stroke, or you can reposition the rod during the drift time for a new position. This exercise focuses on drifting in the same direction of the loop, for a longer casting stroke.

Key concepts:

- Drift is a repositioning of the rod tip after the stop
- Drift is the backward complement to follow through forward
- Drift time is used to reposition the rod, either in a new casting plane, for a change of direction, or to reposition the rod further back for a longer forward casting stroke
- Drift is optional, it is not an essential part of the casting stroke
- Fills the void of waiting time while your back cast unrolls
- Smoothes out the cast by keeping you in contact with the line as it unrolls
- Drift is without power
- For a longer stroke, the direction of drift is along the same trajectory of the cast
- Drift in the vertical plane is up and back, watch the elbow lift
- Drift in the off vertical plane is out and back, watch the elbow leave your side
- Maximum drift angle using body structure: off vertical is 90° angle from under side of forearm to side of body, and 90° from upper arm to forearm
- Forward cast starts with the elbow returning close to the body, this begins the loading

Back cast
- ☐ Closed stance
- ☐ Make the back cast
- ☐ After the stop allow the line to fall
- ☐ Find a fixed object in the practice area and note the position of the rod tip relative to this object
- ☐ Reposition the rod tip further back along the straight line of the cast
- ☐ Note the rod tip movement relative to your fixed object
- ☐ Note the elbow movement after the drift, the elbow lifts in the closed stance
- ☐ Use body structure to guide maximum drift length
- ☐ Pause and evaluate the rod arm position

Forward cast
- ☐ Begin with elbow lowering down in the closed stance
- ☐ Continue trajectory for forward cast
- ☐ Aim cast with thumb pad, lining up opposite target
- ☐ Wrist rotation on the stop
- ☐ Follow through forward and deliver the cast

Start your practice with small amounts of drift, only a few inches. Practice to develop a range of drift movements: short, medium and long to match the length of line cast.

Practice the drift technique using these practice exercises:
- Isolating the back cast
- Rod arm mechanics pantomime
- Open stance, off vertical position

Photo series 60- top: vertical position drift, note rod tip repositioned and , elbow lifts; bottom: forward cast, note elbow has lowered

Rod Arm Mechanics: Off Vertical with Drift

Use this exercise indoors or outside with your full rod. If indoors, use a mirror and your practice rod. Stand side ways to the mirror, to watch your rod arm travel on a straight line both during the cast and during the drift move. If you are outside, use just your rod arm. Have the 40-foot mark of your line at the rod tip. Use the open stance and a hip rotation for the off vertical position. Make the back cast following your checklist. Find the stop first, and then add drift. Make all the movements slowly so you can watch and feel the sequence of body movements as you cast. Be sure to watch the direction of your rod arm movement on the drift. Be sure to drift in a direction to follow the unrolling loop. After making several individual back casts with drift, begin false casting with drift.

Key concepts:
- Use a straight line in the practice area as a guide for your straight line cast
- Open stance position
- Hand and forearm rotate to the off vertical position as you start to lift the line
- Hip/body rotation on first back cast to facilitate straight path of rod tip
- Rod hand and arm stop in front or even with shoulder
- Drift back on a straight line toward imaginary loop of line, elbow leaves your side
- Do not drift beyond 90° angles of upper arm to body and upper arm to forearm
- Forward cast starts with elbow moving back toward your side
- Forward cast continues in the off vertical casting plane
- False cast in the open stance
- Hip/body rotation back toward target on delivery cast
- Hip rotation can add speed by using momentum of the rotation
- Delivery cast is made in same casting plane, check thumb and wrist for casting plane
- Add follow through forward when false casting
- Use body structure to make the cast:
  - Body block to stop the rod
  - Body rotation to facilitate longer stroke and add acceleration to the cast
  - Arm structure for maximum drift: 90° angles of upper arm to body and upper arm to forearm (use angles as a guideline)

Practice the off vertical and drift techniques using these practice exercises:
- Rod arm mechanics exercise to practice the off vertical position
- Isolating the back cast
- Accuracy
- Straight line casting

Off vertical with drift

- ☐ Start back cast:
    - o Use the open stance
    - o Elbow at hip level
    - o Hand is relaxed
    - o Wrist in the bent down position
- ☐ Making the cast:
    - o Forearm lifts back toward body
    - o Forearm and hand are rotated outward slightly, placing the rod at an angle
    - o Elbow is close to your side, forearm is angled out from your body
    - o Cast is made on a straight line trajectory toward your back cast target area
    - o Hips rotate to allow rod to move in a straight line (body rotation)
    - o Body block can be used to help stop the rod
    - o Hand squeezes tight on the back cast stop, then relaxes
- ☐ End the cast:
    - o Thumb is upright, not pointed down
    - o Rod butt is 30°- 45° angle from the underside of your forearm
    - o Hips and shoulders are sideways to target
    - o Forearm and hand stop in front or even with shoulder
    - o Hand maintains off vertical angle
    - o Hand is now relaxed
    - o Drift back and upward, toward the unrolling loop
    - o Use body structure to guide longer drifts
    - o Long drift position is 90° angle from upper arm to body and 90° angle from forearm to upper arm (may adjust as you develop skill with drift)
    - o Elbow leaves your side
- ☐ Start forward cast:
    - o Hand is relaxed, no tension
    - o Look at your target so you can aim your cast
    - o Wrist is in the straight position at an off vertical angle
    - o Rod butt is 30°- 45° from forearm
    - o Elbow leads and returns to your side (after drift)
- ☐ Making the cast:
    - o Elbow starts forward acceleration
    - o Maintain the angle of the rod butt, no change in wrist position
    - o Move your hand on a straight line toward your target
    - o Hips return to start position without force, after the forearm is in front of your hips
    - o Thumb pad lines up directly opposite target
    - o Wrist rotation on the stop: thumb pushes forward while lower fingers pull back
    - o Hand has tension during the stop, holds for a moment and then relaxes
- ☐ End forward cast:
    - o Wrist is in the bent down position
    - o Rod butt is parallel with forearm

- o Hand is relaxed
- o Lower rod tip during follow through time
- o Elbow returns to your hip level
- o Follow through forward if false casting

Photo series 61 Top: L-R: off vertical start position, then stop; bottom: L-R: off vertical drift then forward cast

Longer Casting Stroke

When casting longer lengths of the line, a longer stroke is required. You need a longer casting stroke to move the longer line. Forearm to the upper arm is the maximum stroke length of your arm. Add body movement for additional stroke length.

Key concepts:
- Longer line length requires a longer stroke
- Longer stroke allows for smooth acceleration of the longer line
- Accelerating over a longer distance yields a deeper bend in the rod: more energy for the cast
- Add body movement to increase stroke length

Set up
- ☐ Use open or closed stance, right foot dropped back
- ☐ Bend left knee
- ☐ Lean forward, weight is on left foot
- ☐ Use a point on the ground as reference to see the increased stroke length resulting from the increased body movement

Back cast
- ☐ While starting the back cast stroke: shift weight from left foot to right foot
- ☐ End back cast with weight on the right foot
- ☐ Cast unrolls

Forward cast
- ☐ While beginning the forward casting stroke, shift weight from right foot to left foot
- ☐ End the forward cast with weight on the left foot
- ☐ Cast unrolls

Practice false casting with a weight shift in each direction. Focus on the weight shift as helping you slowly begin the casting stroke acceleration. The weight shift should increase the overall stroke length. Watch your body position relative to a point on the ground. You should see an increase in the lateral distance you move when adding body movement.

Practice the longer stroke technique using these practice exercises:
- Rod arm mechanics
- Isolating the cast
- Continuous false casting
- Horizontal casting

217

Photo series 62- top: - rock forward for longer back cast stroke; bottom: - rock backward for a longer forward cast stroke

Casting Arc

To maintain a straight line path of the rod tip, the more deeply loaded rod requires a wider casting arc. The casting arc is the angle of the rod butt from the beginning of the cast to the end of the cast.

Key concepts:
- Stroke length and casting arc must be matched to the length of line you are casting
- Casting longer lines creates a deeper load in the rod (more weight to bend the rod)
- A longer stroke creates a deeper bend in the rod, providing more energy for the cast
- To keep the rod tip moving in a straight line, the casting arc must widen

Back cast
- ☐ Start in the open stance, off vertical position
- ☐ Use body movement to lift the line and make a back cast
- ☐ After the stop, drift back with the rod tip
- ☐ During drift relax and allow your arm to leave your side
- ☐ Note the rod butt position after the drift, this is the beginning of your wider arc for the forward cast

Forward cast
- ☐ Elbow returns to your side as you begin the acceleration of the forward casting stroke
- ☐ Smoothly accelerate with the longer stroke
- ☐ Aim your cast
- ☐ Move your rod arm and line up your thumb pad opposite the target area
- ☐ Begin the wrist rotation to a stop, while still moving forward through the stroke
- ☐ After the stop, note the rod butt position, this is the end of your casting arc
- ☐ Your casting arc should be wider when casting longer lengths of line
- ☐ Follow through forward if false casting
- ☐ Continue false casting using drift backward and follow through forward or present your cast

Practice the casting arc technique using these practice exercises:
- Horizontal casting and its variations
- Isolating each cast
- Continuous false casting

Photo series 63- wider arc for casting longer line

Advanced Casting Techniques: Lesson 3: Distance Casting

Distance casting requires fine-tuning your basic casting abilities. To cast distance you need to be efficient and ensure all efforts contribute toward the cast. For distance, the main areas of focus are loading and unloading the rod; forming tight, aerodynamic loops; increasing stroke length; and refining the double haul. The final component to casting maximum distance is shooting line on the final back cast. Add this technique only after you have improved the basic components of distance casting.

This practice section highlights specific areas of focus within each casting technique that are critical to distance casting. Distance magnifies any imperfections in your casting, so minor adjustments can have major benefits to the cast. Start by reviewing the details of your basic casting techniques. Utilize the practice techniques from the first two lessons. When you have solid fundamentals, you can progress to focus on the concepts that will help you cast distance.

For distance practice, use 40 feet of line at the rod tip. With a nine foot rod you are casting 49 feet of line plus your leader for a total of 58 feet. Begin your practice in the sequence presented outlined below. Use the basic casting exercises to work on your fundamentals and then focus on the nuisances for distance casting.

- ☐ Casting Techniques:
- ☐ Loading & unloading the rod: back cast and forward cast
- ☐ Lengthening the casting stroke with drift
- ☐ Tight loops
- ☐ Double Haul
- ☐ False casting longer lines
- ☐ Shooting line on the last back cast

Loading and Unloading the rod

The heart of any fly cast is the bending and unbending of the rod. Accomplishing this efficiently requires attention to detail. By isolating each cast, you can make a series of just back or forward casts and work exclusively on your area of focus for that practice session. Then you can rebuild your cast, fine-tuning your skills and developing new muscle memory to solidify your new skills.

Isolating the back cast: basic back cast mechanics
- ☐ Start position
- ☐ Start with the line straight in front of you and no slack line
- ☐ Place your rod tip low to the grass this allows you to start loading the rod immediately
- ☐ Stand in the closed stance, with your shoulders square to the target
- ☐ Begin with the vertical casting plane: forearm in line with your upper arm, facilitating moving in a straight line
- ☐ Wrist in the bent down position, rod butt is parallel with forearm
- ☐ Hand relaxed
- ☐ Use the thumb on top grip
- ☐ Trajectory of the back cast is back and up; make the cast unroll over an imaginary fence behind you
- ☐ Start the lifting of the line by using your entire forearm and hand
- ☐ Lift your forearm up on a diagonal path toward your temple
- ☐ You can see and feel your elbow rise, this ensures an upward as well as backward line trajectory
- ☐ Be sure your wrist stays in the bent down position during the lifting of the line
- ☐ Use just enough acceleration to lift the line, the rod will bend under this weight
- ☐ The lift ends when you reach the line leader connection (end of the loading phase)
- ☐ Stop the rod by squeezing your rod hand tightly and tightening the muscles in your arm to cease all motion (unloading the rod)
- ☐ Relax your hand
- ☐ Hold the back cast stop position and evaluate your position: thumb is upright, rod butt is 30°- 45° angle to forearm, forearm is in front of upper arm, elbow has lifted, and hand has no tension
- ☐ Allow the cast to fall to the ground behind you
- ☐ Lower the rod tip to the ground behind you
- ☐ Turn around in place to face your just landed back cast
- ☐ Take a few steps backwards to remove slack line
- ☐ Make another back cast
- ☐ Off vertical casting plane uses the open stance: tilt elbow in and forearm out, turn your head to watch the cast

Use this exercise to focus on:
- Rod arm Mechanics
- Change in wrist positions from the start of the cast to the end of the cast

- Using the body block for an abrupt stop
- Rate of acceleration of the back cast lift
- Application of power on the stop
- Tight loops and straight line casting
- Developing your back cast haul, double and single
- Shooting line on the back cast
- Aiming the back cast
- Practice making the back cast in different casting planes

Back cast with focus on distance: loading and unloading the rod
- ☐ Start in the vertical position to use your body structure to facilitate moving in a straight line
- ☐ Hand is relaxed
- ☐ Wrist is in the bent down position
- ☐ Start with no slack line, rod tip should be just above the grass
- ☐ Aim the back cast
- ☐ Focus on smooth acceleration as you lift the line, do not pull the rod with your hand and wrist, lift with your forearm
- ☐ Lift the forearm and hand as a unit, with the rod butt parallel to the forearm
- ☐ Lift until the line-leader connection is reached
- ☐ Squeeze the rod butt on the stop, and then relax your hand
- ☐ Maximum stroke length uses your body structure to help with the stop: body block
- ☐ After the stop check the position of the thumbnail, the imaginary line should be at the horizon
- ☐ Off vertical: use the open stance
- ☐ Hip rotation is used to facilitate straight line path of the rod
- ☐ Need a relaxed hand and arm to feel the rod load throughout the stroke

Practice exercises:
- Isolate the back cast
- Use the details of arm position for the back cast (see basic cast and rod arm mechanics practice)
- Use body structure to help stop the rod
- Aim the back cast exercise
- Off vertical and open stance rod arm mechanics exercise
- Focus on hand tension only on the stops, use the sponge practice exercise

Photo series 64-top: start with rod tip low, hold position, after the stop, allow line to fall and evaluate arm mechanics ; bottom: thumb aims the cast, note angle of rod butt to forearm

<u>Isolating the forward cast</u>: basic forward cast mechanics
Forward cast:
- ☐ Start position
- ☐ Start by making a back cast and allowing the line to fall behind you
- ☐ Walk forward a few steps to remove any slack line
- ☐ Stand in the closed stance, with your shoulders square to the target
- ☐ Begin with the vertical casting plane: forearm in line with your upper arm, facilitating moving in a straight line
- ☐ Wrist in the straight position, rod butt is 45 ° to forearm
- ☐ Hand is relaxed
- ☐ Use the thumb on top grip, thumb is upright
- ☐ Trajectory of the forward cast is along an imaginary diagonal line toward the target
- ☐ Start the acceleration by leading with the elbow (feel the elbow lower, in vertical plane)
- ☐ Accelerate through the casting stroke sequence: upper arm, forearm, and hand, dragging the line forward (not pushing)
- ☐ Be sure your wrist stays in the straight position during loading of the rod
- ☐ Use just enough acceleration to move the fly line toward your target, creating a bend in the rod
- ☐ Move your rod hand forward until your thumb pad is opposite the target (the rod is loaded)
- ☐ Stop the rod by squeezing your rod hand: push forward with your thumb, while pulling back with the lower fingers for the wrist rotation of the stop
- ☐ Relax your hand
- ☐ Hold the forward cast stop position and evaluate your position: wrist is in the bent down position, rod butt is parallel with forearm (0°), hand is relaxed
- ☐ Watch the loop unroll and allow the cast to fall to the ground
- ☐ Lower the rod tip to the ground
- ☐ Turn around in place to face the opposite direction
- ☐ Raise the rod tip up, so you are in the starting position
- ☐ Take a few steps forward to remove slack line
- ☐ Make another forward cast
- ☐ Off vertical casting plane uses the open stance: tilt elbow in and forearm out, turn your head to watch the cast

Use this exercise to focus on:
- Rod arm mechanics
- Change in wrist positions from the start of the cast to the end of the cast
- Use of the forward cast wrist rotation for an abrupt stop
- Rate of acceleration of the forward cast
- Application of power on the stop
- Tight loops and straight line casting
- Developing your forward cast hauls, single and double
- Shooting line on your forward cast
- Aiming the forward cast
- Practice making the back cast in different casting planes

Forward cast with focus on distance: <u>load and unloading the rod</u>

- ☐ Start in the vertical position
- ☐ Hand is relaxed
- ☐ Rod butt is 45° angle to the forearm
- ☐ Start with no slack line
- ☐ Look forward to aim the cast
- ☐ Focus on smooth acceleration to the stop: applying abrupt power yields a tailing loop
- ☐ Sequence of arm movement is important: elbow leads, then forearm, lastly the hand
- ☐ Forward cast should feel like you are dragging the line from behind you
- ☐ Arm movement is like a baseball throw: move the rod to create a bend, lining up with the target area and use wrist rotation at the end of the stroke to stop the rod
- ☐ Wrist rotation unloads the rod, forcing it out of the bend and releases energy into the fly line
- ☐ Off vertical uses the open stance
- ☐ Hip rotation to facilitate the straight line path of the rod
- ☐ Hip rotation can also add speed as you swivel back to forward position
- ☐ Wrist rotation to a stop adds power to the cast, it completes the rod loading and stops the rod (load to unload)
- ☐ Aim for a longer cast trajectory
- ☐ Lower the rod tip at the rate the unrolling loop is falling to the ground
- ☐ Use a relaxed hand and arm to feel the rod load throughout the stroke
- ☐ Avoid the tendency to overpower the rod, do not add force to the final forward cast

Practice exercises:
- Isolate the forward cast
- Use details of arm position for the forward cast: see basic cast and rod arm mechanics practice
- Focus on hand tension only on the stops, use the sponge practice exercise
- Use horizontal casting exercise and focus on smooth loading of the rod, and practice a range of acceleration rates
- Use horizontal casting and the casting form to focus on how the wrist rotation of the stop triggers the unloading of the rod
- Off vertical and open stance rod arm mechanics exercise
- Horizontal casting alone and with the casting form and using straight lines

Photo series 65-top: forward cast, vertical stance: start position; mid: stop ; bottom: hold position and evaluate arm mechanics

Photo series 66- top: L:-R- forward cast off vertical stance, start position, stop and evaluate rod arm position; bottom: L-R- wrist rotate on the stop; follow through as line falls to grass

Lengthen the Casting Stroke with Drift

To more deeply load the rod and travel in a straight path you need to increase the stroke length. You will use body movement, drift and follow through. Drift is a repositioning of the rod tip after the stop. It allows for a longer forward casting stroke.

Lengthen the casting stroke: basic technique

When casting longer lengths of the line, a longer stroke is required. You need a longer casting stroke to move the longer line. Forearm to the upper arm is the maximum stroke length of your arm. Add body movement for additional stroke length.

Basic concepts:
- Longer line length requires a longer stroke
- Longer stroke allows for smooth acceleration of longer line
- Accelerating over a longer distance yields a deeper bend in the rod and more energy for the cast
- Add body movement to increase stroke length

Set up
- ☐ Use open or closed stance, right foot dropped back
- ☐ Bend left knee
- ☐ Lean forward, weight is on left foot
- ☐ Use a reference point on the ground to measure your stroke length with body movement added

Back cast stroke length
- ☐ While starting the back cast stroke, shift weight from left foot to right foot
- ☐ End back cast with weight on the right foot
- ☐ Cast unrolls

Forward cast stroke length
- ☐ While beginning the forward casting stroke, shift weight from right foot to left foot
- ☐ End the forward cast with weight on the left foot
- ☐ Cast unrolls

Practice false casting with a weight shift in each direction. Focus on the weight shift as helping you slowly begin the casting stroke acceleration. The weight shift should increase the overall stroke length. Watch your body position relative to a point on the ground: you should see an increase in lateral distance you move when adding body movement.

Lengthen the casting stroke with Drift : basic technique:

Back cast
- ☐ Closed stance
- ☐ Make the back cast
- ☐ After the stop, allow the line to fall
- ☐ Find a fixed object in the practice area and note the position of the rod tip relative to this object
- ☐ Reposition the rod tip further back along the straight line

☐ Note the rod tip movement relative to your fixed object
☐ Note the elbow movement after the drift, your elbow leaves your side
☐ Use body structure to guide maximum drift length
☐ Pause and evaluate your rod arm position

Forward cast
☐ Begins with elbow returning to your side for off vertical position, elbow lowers with the closed stance
☐ Continue trajectory of the forward cast
☐ Aim cast with thumb pad, lining up opposite target
☐ Wrist rotation on the stop
☐ Follow through forward and deliver the cast

Drift technique for distance:
Key concepts:
☐ To cast more distance you need more load in the rod, to transfer more energy to the loop allowing more line to be shot
☐ Deeper load in the rod must still be developed gradually and smoothly
☐ Drift is done after the stop
☐ Drift is without power
☐ Repositions the rod tip for a longer casting stroke and keeps you connected to the feeling of tension as the loop unrolls
☐ Drift continues the lateral movement of the rod
☐ Use open stance and off vertical position
☐ Use a body rotation to accommodate the rod arm movement of a longer stroke
☐ Use the body block (body structure to stop the rod before drift)
☐ Need a wider casting arc: relax during drift and allow rod butt angle to open slightly
☐ Practice a range of drifts
☐ Drift amount should be matched to the length of line being cast: develop a range of drift lengths
☐ Increase forearm to upper arm angle cautiously on your longest drift
☐ Allow elbow to move away from body during drift
☐ Next forward cast begins with the elbow moving back, close to the body, it is a re-collecting of the rod arm back to its initial stop position

Practice exercises:
• Off vertical rod arm mechanics practice
• Casting form to find the space for drift, outside of the casting stroke, after the stop
• Horizontal casting exercise
• Pantomime rod arm mechanics with mirror
• Practice single back and forward cast, then false casting
• Start with small amounts of drift, only a few inches.
• Practice to develop a range of drift movements: short, medium and long to match the length of line being cast

Photo series 68-stop first, then drift

Photo series 67- forward cast, elbow returns to side

Tight Loops

To get tight loops the rod tip must travel in a straight path. This is the fundamental principle to forming tight loops. To allow the more deeply loaded rod to travel in a straight path you need widen the casting arc. Focus on straight line casting. Build a greater rod load smoothly by lengthening the stroke and adjusting the casting arc. Incorporate all of these elements and you will form tight loops for longer casts.

Visual Straight Line casting exercise: tight loop basics:
Use the horizontal casting exercise with a line to improve your ability to cast along a straight line. Place your rod tip close to this line and use the line as a guide for the straight line path.

Basic concepts:
- Using a visual straight line facilitates the straight line path movement of your rod arm
- The entire casting stroke (loading move and wrist rotation), drift and follow through occur along this straight line
- Focus on the rod tip along the rope, your elbow leaves your side on drift and follow through
- Elbow is close to your side on the stop positions
- Horizontal casting allows you to watch the cast and see the loop size and shape

Straight line casting exercise: Set up is similar to the horizontal casting, with a rope between the targets
- ☐ Back cast
  - o Start with rod arm extended slightly to the left
  - o Elbow moves toward body at beginning of casting stroke
  - o Rod tip moves along the rope
  - o Elbow is close to your side during the stop
- ☐ Drift: occurs after the stop
  - o Reposition the rod tip along the straight line path (maintains the loop shape)
- ☐ Forward cast
  - o Begin with elbow returning back to your side
  - o Rod tip moves along the rope during the casting stroke
  - o Elbow is close to your side on the stop
- ☐ Follow through: occurs after the stop
  - o Reposition the rod tip forward, along the straight line to maintain loop shape
- ☐ False casting
  - o Elbow moves to facilitate the straight line path of the rod tip
    - ▪ Elbow must move away from your body on drift and follow through
    - ▪ Elbow returns to your body on the loading move in both directions
    - ▪ Elbow is close to your side during the stops
- ☐ Casting arc
  - o Watch the stop position of rod butt on both back cast and forward cast
  - o The stop positions show you the casting arc
  - o Too wide of an arc yields a wide loop

        o   Too narrow of an arc yields a closed, tailing loop

      Make a series of back and forward casts. Move through the casting stroke slowly. Focus on the path your rod arm takes to maintain the rod tip along the straight line. Notice that if you move too close to the straight line, your cast will be above the line. You must stand a rod length away from the rope in order to cast along the straight line. False cast a series of 3-4 false casts. Focus on the rod tip moving along the straight line and the movement of your rod arm to ensure this straight line path. Remember to check your rod butt to forearm angles and wrist positions at the beginning and end of each cast.

Casting arc basics: false casting
<u>False casting practice</u>
- ☐ While false casting:
- ☐ Watch your loop size, if loops are big you are moving in a wide arc, curved pattern
- ☐ Tighten the casting arc for more narrow loops
- ☐ If you get a tailing loop, the casting arc is too narrow and needs to widen
- ☐ Watch the angle of the rod butt on the stops to monitor the casting arc

<u>Casting arc for distance:</u>
Key concepts:
- Casting longer lines creates a deeper load in the rod
- A longer stroke creates a deeper bend in the rod
- To keep the rod tip moving in a straight line, the casting arc must widen

Back cast
- ☐ Start in the open stance, off vertical position and lean forward
- ☐ Use body movement to help lift the line
- ☐ After the stop drift back with the rod
- ☐ During drift relax, and allow your arm to leave your side
- ☐ Note the rod butt position after the drift, this is the beginning of your wider arc for the forward cast

Forward cast
- ☐ Elbow returns to your side as you begin the acceleration of the forward casting stroke
- ☐ Smoothly accelerate with the longer stroke
- ☐ Aim the cast
- ☐ Move your rod arm forward lining up your thumb pad opposite the target area
- ☐ Begin the wrist rotation to a stop on the trajectory to the target
- ☐ Follow through forward when false casting
- ☐ Note the rod butt position after the stop, this is the end of your casting arc
- ☐ Your casting arc should be wider when casting longer lengths of line
- ☐ Continue false casting with drift backward and follow through forward or present your cast

Stroke length and casting arc must be matched to the length of line you are casting. A longer line requires a longer casting stroke to ensure smooth acceleration. The deeper load in the rod requires a wider casting arc to maintain the straight line path of the rod tip.

<u>Tight loops for distance casting:</u>
Key Concepts:
- ☐ Loop size and shape is determined by the path of the rod tip
- ☐ Rod tip must travel on a straight line throughout the casting stroke including the stop
- ☐ Loops should be aimed toward the target
- ☐ Narrow loops are more aerodynamic and contain more energy, are better in the wind and can shoot more line
- ☐ Narrow loops concentrate the line's energy in a narrow area, you can direct this energy to unroll the loop at your target
- ☐ Aim the back as well as the forward cast, it is easier to move in a straight line and narrow loop if you aim your cast
- ☐ Use your thumb as an aiming device: thumb pad for forward cast, and thumbnail for back cast, the imaginary straight line running through your thumb
- ☐ Casting arc must adjust for the amount of bend in the rod, a deeper bend needs a wider arc to facilitate the straight line path of the rod
- ☐ Monitor tracking in a straight line
- ☐ Monitor loop size and shape: too wide an arc yield wide loops, too narrow arc yield tailing loops
- ☐ Lower the rod tip at the rate the unrolling loop is falling to the ground

Practice exercises:
- Aiming the back cast exercise
- Visual straight line and two line exercises to improve tracking
- Use the open stance, off vertical plane and watch your cast
- Monitor the casting arc
- Pantomime with a rod butt and mirror to watch for wider casting arc to maintain straight line path of rod tip
- Continuous false casting to monitor loop size and shape

Photo series 69- straight path of rod tip to target for tight loop

Double Haul

The double haul decreases the effort required to load the rod, increases line speed and helps form a tighter loop. Properly executed, it is a valuable casting technique, done poorly it allows mistakes to be cast farther.

<u>Horizontal casting to practice the double haul</u>, basic double haul technique:
- Double haul is a haul and give back, a two direction move
- Single haul is a one direction move, a haul, with no give back
- Haul is coordinated with the wrist action on the stop
- Length of the haul is matched to the length of the wrist rotation
- Haul is balanced to the cast for speed and power
- Direction of the haul is opposite the rod's movement
- Haul accelerates to a stop, it is a crisp, sharp move
- The give back motion is slower, it occurs at the rate the unrolling loop will accept
- Line hand must be sure there is no slack line
- Monitor the line from the first stripping guide to the line hand; this should always be under tension
- Haul will increase line speed, deepen the load in the rod and form a tighter loop

Set up:
- ☐ Set up is identical to the horizontal casting exercise
- ☐ Be sure to use targets that are placed 180° from each other
- ☐ Use 40 feet of line
- ☐ Allow 2-3 feet of line between hands so you have line to use for hauling

Back cast double haul:
- ☐ Start with a bent down wrist, the rod butt is parallel to forearm
- ☐ Line hand palm is down and in parallel with rod hand
- ☐ Move your line hand and rod hand in unison toward your back cast target
- ☐ Watch the rod begin to load
- ☐ Use your rod arm thumb to aim the back cast
- ☐ When thumbnail is lined up opposite the back cast target, squeeze to a stop
- ☐ The line hand hauls **while** the rod hand executes the stop
- ☐ Line hand accelerates to the left, opposite the rod hand movement
- ☐ The wrist changes to the straight position, the rod butt is now at a 45° angle **and** the haul has ended
- ☐ After the rod stop, move your eyes to the line hand and watch the line for tension as you give back
- ☐ Line hand returns to a position slightly below the reel
- ☐ Allow the cast to fall and evaluate your haul and give back
- ☐ Rest your arm

Forward cast double haul:
☐ Rotate rod arm and line hand to the horizontal position
☐ Rod hand wrist in the straight position (45°angle)
☐ Line hand palm is down, and parallel with rod hand
☐ Move line hand and rod hand in unison toward the forward cast target
☐ Watch the rod begin to bend
☐ Use your thumb to aim the cast
☐ When thumb pad is lined up opposite the forward cast target, begin the wrist rotation
☐ The line hand hauls **while** the rod hand executes the stop
☐ Line hand accelerates toward left hip, opposite the rod hand movement
☐ Wrist angle changes to the bent down position, **and** the haul has ended
☐ After the rod stop, move your eyes to the line hand and watch the line for tension as you give back
☐ Line hand returns to just below the reel
☐ Allow the cast to fall and evaluate your haul and give back
☐

After you have practiced single back and forward casts, false cast with double hauling. Monitor the line in your line hand to be sure there is no slack line. Watch the loop as it unrolls. Give the line back at the rate the unrolling loop will accept. Close your eyes, feel the haul, and give back. Feel the line to be under tension. Open your eyes and move to the vertical position. Make six false casts with double hauling then rest.

Double haul for distance:
Key Concepts:
☐ Perfect your hauling for maximum benefit and avoid slack in the cast
☐ Look for slack prior to the haul
☐ Both hands begin the casting stroke moving in the same direction (you cannot haul until the rod is loaded)
☐ Haul should be in a direction opposite the rod arm movement, it increases line tension
☐ Haul is crisp
☐ Haul is a long as the stop (how long it takes to stop the rod, the haul ends when the rod had stopped)
☐ Watch the line from first stripping guide to your line hand, and be sure it is under tension at all times
☐ Giving back of the line must be matched to the speed of the unrolling loop
☐ Haul hand should return line until the hand is positioned just below the reel: this allows you to maximize the length of the next forward cast haul
☐ Watch to be sure the haul hand is moving away from the rod hand, the rod hand should not pull away from the line hand
☐ Focus on avoiding slack and quality of the haul to increase tension

Practice exercises:
• Horizontal casting exercise and its variations, including the casting form
• Haul with rod under the arm to isolate the line hand functions
• Hauling off the water
• Isolating each cast

Photo series 70- top: - line under tension at start of back cast; mid: line under tension during haul; bottom- line under tension during give back

Photo series 71- top: - line under tension at start of forward cast; mid: line under tension during haul, haul starts after rod loaded; bottom: line under tension at end of haul, and give back

False Cast Longer Lines

False casting: basic technique

      When false casting you are adding the line hand and you must be sure, there is no slack line. Watch the line from your first stripping guide to the line hand and be sure there is no slack. This line should always be under tension.

Basic Concepts:
- Line hand has responsibility to be sure there is no slack line in the cast
- Line hand pinches the line during the cast
- Line hand is positioned slightly lower and apart from the reel
- Line hand moves in unison, parallel with the rod hand
- Line hand lifts and lowers to follow the rod hand movements
- Forward cast is not allowed to touch the water when false casting
- Trajectory changes to allow the cast to unroll above the target
- Opportunity to work on timing between casts
- Anticipate the cast fully unrolling: watch for candy cane shape at the end of loop, this is your cue to start the next cast
- Hand tension only on the stops, hand is relaxed during the casting stroke
- Loop control, watch loop size and adjust casting arc for good loop
- Use all three parts of your arm while false casting

      While false casting, focus on having an oval shaped loop. The stops should be crisp on both the back and forward casts. Monitor your timing. Listen for the sound of your line as it unrolls. There should be no cracks or whip noises. Use enough speed to keep the cast aloft. Relax between the stops while you false cast. Limit false casting to a series of four casts to keep focused.

False casting basic practice
- ☐ Strip off two feet of line so you have room for both hands to move
- ☐ Line hand pinches the line between thumb and index finger
- ☐ Make the back cast
- ☐ Watch the line to be sure there is no slack between your line hand and first stripping guide
- ☐ Aim the forward cast several feet above the target
- ☐ Do not let your cast hit the water in front
- ☐ Watch your loop size, if they are big you are moving in a wide arc, curved pattern
- ☐ Tighten the casting arc, for more narrow loops
- ☐ If you get a tailing loop, the casting arc is too narrow and needs to widen
- ☐ Watch the angle of the rod butt on the stops to monitor the casting arc
- ☐ Monitor rod arm movements: forearm moves back and forth, elbow lifts and lowers, wrist opens and closes
- ☐ Must have a loading move before the stop or you get a tailing loop
- ☐ Watch your loops unroll in front of you and anticipate when the loop is almost unrolled

□ Look for the loop to resemble the hook of a candy cane this is your cue to start the next cast
□ Listen to your timing between casts there should be no cracking noises
□ Relax your hand between casts to feel the rod butt stop vibrating for good timing
□ Tension only on the stops, no tension within the casting stroke

<u>False casting longer lines for distance:</u>

Key concepts
□ Need longer stroke length to build the deeper load smoothly
□ Use drift and follow through
□ Adjust timing and allow back cast to straighten completely
□ Trajectory for false casting longer lines: allow cast to unroll completely and then fall slightly so the next cast can have an upward trajectory

Practice exercises:
• Horizontal casting and variations
• Continuous false casting

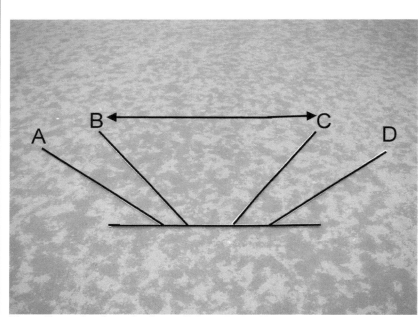

Photo 63--casting form: <u>back cast</u> R-L: A-B - loading move ; B-C - stop/wrist rotation; C-D – drift; <u>forward cast</u>: L-R: D-C- loading move; C-B- stop/wrist rotation; B-A-follow through

Photo series 72- top: L-R- stop, then drift setting up for longer forward cast stroke; bottom: L-R- stop, then follow through forward for longer back cast stroke

Shooting Line on Last Back Cast

Shooting line: basic technique

      Planning your false casts and line shooting can eliminate excessive false casting. Understanding your fly line design helps you maximize your plan for casting and shooting line.

Basic concepts:
- Line can be shot on both the forward and back cast
- Need line outside of rod tip to provide weight to pull additional line with the shoot
- Line shot is pulled by the energy in the loop of fly line
- Efficient unloading of the rod provides energy in the loop
- Loop must form before you can shoot line
- Line hand alternately pinches and releases the line
- Maximum line shoot is determined by the casters ability to control the line, and the line design: excess avoid overhang
- Minimize false casting and plan the line shoot

Shooting line basic practice

Set up:
- ☐ Start with 40 feet of line (40 foot line marking in your hand)
- ☐ Strip an additional 10 feet of line for shooting
- ☐ Be sure the line is stretched to remove coils

Back cast
- ☐ Use either closed or open stance
- ☐ Use rod hand and line hand
- ☐ Start with line straight in front of you
- ☐ Make a back cast
- ☐ Focus on the abrupt stop
- ☐ After the back cast stop, while the loop is unrolling, shoot a few inches of line
- ☐ Pinch the line to stop the shoot
- ☐ Allow loop to almost unroll
- ☐ Begin forward cast

Forward cast
- ☐ Continue the forward casting stroke
- ☐ Aim the forward cast
- ☐ When thumb pad is positioned opposite the forward cast target area, begin the wrist rotation to a stop
- ☐ Watch for the loop to form
- ☐ Release line and shoot a few inches
- ☐ Pinch the line to stop the shoot
- ☐ Allow loop to unroll and deliver the cast

When you are comfortable with the pinching and releasing of line, try shooting line on each cast. Be careful not to be exceed your ability to control the longer length of line.

<u>Shooting line for distance:</u> the final back cast shoot

Key concepts:

- ☐ Maximum line to false cast is the head of the fly line
- ☐ Need extra energy in the loop to be able to shoot line
- ☐ Use body structure for an abrupt stop
- ☐ Shooting extra line on final back cast preloads the rod so greater load is achieved
- ☐ Can shoot to lengthen the line beyond the head length
- ☐ Only exceed casting with more than the head length on the final back cast

Practice exercises:

- Isolate the cast when learning to shoot line on back cast. Adjust timing and learn to feel the tug of the line completely straightening
- Practice the line hand alternately pinching and releasing line
- Practice a single false cast with back cast shoot, allow line to fall
- Practice shooting on the final back cast and delivering the next forward cast

Photo series 73- use body structure to help stop rod, and shoot line on back cast for pre-load of rod

Conclusion

By now, you realize that fly casting is more than just fishing. It is a unique skill. It requires time and effort to perfect. Like most valuable and memorable things in life, your practice with fly casting will repay you with a lifetime of challenges, memories of wonderful places and time you spend fishing.

I hope you reach your potential and learn to maximize and enjoy each cast. I wish you tight lines and perfect casts!

Index